Talking With The

ANIMALS

PATTY SUMMERS

Talking With The
ANIMALS

HAMPTON ROADS
PUBLISHING COMPANY, INC.

Text illustrations by Linda Oberlender

Cover art by the following photographers through Index Stock Photgraphy:

John Dominis	Bruce Ando
Kathy Heister	Vic Bider
Lela Tinstman	Peter Adams
Frank Staub	James Church
Elizabeth DeLaney	Gay Bumgarner

Cover design by Marjoram Productions

For information write:

Hampton Roads Publishing Company, Inc.
134 Burgess Lane
Charlottesville, VA 22902

Or call: 804-296-2772
Fax: 804-296-5096
E-mail: hrpc@hrpub.com
Web site: http://www.hrpub.com

If you are unable to order this book from your local
bookseller, you may order directly from the publisher.
Quantity discounts for organizations are available.
Call 1-800-766-8009, toll-free.

Library of Congress Catalog Card Number: 98-71584

ISBN 1-57174-108-9

10 9 8 7 6 5 4 3 2

Printed on recycled acid-free paper in Canada

DEDICATION

To the two-legged, the four-legged, the
many-legged, those that burrow, those
that crawl, those that swim, those that
fly, the stone people, and the plant
people. For it is for you that I walked
the wind to deliver your message.

TABLE OF CONTENTS

ACKNOWLEDGMENTS

Thank you, Father/Mother God, Great Spirit.

I wish to thank Ereenie for sharing with me peace and a sense of stability. To Freeman, for sharing strength, courage, and a sense of leadership. Squeaky, for sharing your cat medicine, I honor your graceful wild spirit. I acknowledge Sassyfras, for reminding me to have fun. Kallee, I am in deep gratitude that you have come to share your words of wisdom. Mauvree, my beloved companion, you share dog medicine at its finest. Our hearts shall always be connected. I acknowledge C.C., my great teacher of self-assuredness and acceptance. Thanks to Pethee and Malcom for sharing the gift of innocence. To Ezra, for reminding me of second chances. Ms. Goat and Rosie, thanks for sharing your sassy energy and strength. Zeke, I honor your courage. Popagolis, I thank you for choosing to live with us and for the many lessons that you bring. Quasar, I thank you for opening your heart. To the fish, thank you for the beauty you bring. To Becky Hibbard: yes, angels do exist; thank you for being one of mine. Thanks to David Maurer, for your comments encouraged me to write this book. Thanks to Linda Oberlender for illustrating *Talking with the Animals*. Thank you to those whose stories contributed to the book. Some of your names have been changed to protect your privacy.

Finally, I wish to thank my human partner Joe for loving me and supporting me on my journey.

"In the beginning of all things, wisdom and knowledge were with the animals; for Tirawa, The One Above, did not speak directly to man. He sent animals to tell man that He showed Himself through the beasts, and that from the stars, and the sun, and the moon, man should learn...for all things speak of the Tirawa."

—Pawnee tribe chief Leetakots-Lesa

BEGINNINGS

Anyone can communicate with animals. Telepathic animal communication is not something new; it has been going on for ages in many different cultures. So what is telepathic communication? My definition is that it is the universal language that we all share as brothers and sisters on the Earth Mother. It is the foundation for all language.

Telepathic communication often comes in the form of seeing, hearing, knowing, and/or feeling. For example, a person may receive a thought in the form of a picture. A person may actually hear in his or her mind a thought with words. Many people relate to a "knowing" or "feeling." I will often hear someone say, "I knew that was what my dog wanted," or, "I had a feeling that was what was going on."

At one of my communication workshops I asked the participants to share any personal experiences with telepathic animal communication. One woman told us that she was reading a book when she had the feeling that someone was watching her. She lowered her book to find her Australian shepherd mix sitting in front of her, staring. She told us, "I knew he wanted me to turn the fan on, so I did; then I went back to reading my book. It was a few minutes after I started reading that I realized what had just happened. I lowered my book again to see my dog lying on the floor contentedly as the fan blew across his body."

I have been intuitively interacting with the animals since childhood. As long as I can remember I knew I was to work with animals. So for a number of years I worked in the animal care field. Because telepathic communication was not an accepted practice, for a brief time in my life I pushed my intuitive abilities aside. I found each of my animal-related occupations rewarding and educational, yet there was always something missing. There was a promise deep within, a part of me waiting to be lived. I was to incorporate my ability to communicate with the animals into my work. After reading *Kinship with All Life,* by J. Allen Boone, a book about the author's experiences with telepathic animal communication, I was finally able to step out and walk and talk with conviction of the heart.

I am but a messenger. *Talking with the Animals* is their gift of their wisdom and insights.

DON'T JUDGE A BOOK

The room was constructed of all concrete, walls and floors. There were no windows and the chain-link fencing gave it the effect of a prison cell. Stagnant air and the fluorescent lighting added to the appropriateness of naming this room Isolation. This part of the humane society was reserved for dogs who had just come in and had not been checked over for health and temperament or, more often, for those who were considered unadoptable.

Unadoptable meant they were either unhealthy or had aggressive personalities. I was standing near Iso (as we had nicknamed the room), when I felt someone intently watching me. There he stood, "Cujo" himself. I felt I'd been transported into a Stephen King story. Well, he wasn't the same breed as Cujo, but aside from that he could have played the part well. He was a chow chow, a little large for the breed. He had reddish hair that looked as if dust had been rubbed into his coat, dulling the brightness of the red. The scowl on his face reflected the brutality of his background; in his eyes a look of the wild, a look of utter confidence and self-reliance.

This must be the dog the animal wardens had been talking about earlier. I had worked in several different animal care occupations, including once being an animal control officer myself, so I had seen numerous dogs that other people considered vicious. It wasn't often that I carried the same opinion. My heart went out to these dogs because, usually, there was a reason for their behavior, and quite often it had to do with a human's treatment of them. This dog, however, had strength and power coming through that didn't elicit my heart's compassion. I found myself in fear. I stood frozen for a moment, until I became fully conscious that he was locked in a secure area.

He stared at me, his head lowered just a touch. Once I relaxed a bit, the communication began. "I know you can understand me," the message came. I was dumbfounded. I had just met this dog, actually just laid eyes on him. How did he know I could understand him? I hesitated, then communicated to him, "Ah, yes, that is correct." What's next, I wondered. I was expecting something profound or enlightening. Instead I got, "I need to go outside to relieve myself." The reply was matter-of-fact. I didn't answer; I just walked away. What on earth does he think I am going to do about this? Is he crazy? I'm not taking that dog outside. I know his type. Even if I'm lucky enough to get a leash on him without getting bit, he'll attack me once I get him outside. No way am I. . . . I stopped my mind's chatter. "Hey Patty," I said to myself, "aren't you the one who said you wanted to devote your life's work to animal communication? Aren't you the person who made a commitment to utilizing and trusting your abilities to their fullest?" I knew this was the Universe's way of saying to me: you want it, then show me. Only minutes later, I found myself standing in front of the dog's run. One thing the animals had taught me was the need to be honest. Animals receive my intent, not my words. A lot can be said for animals being good judges of character. They see the real you and the real meaning behind your words.

"Listen," I said, "I am afraid of you. You present an aggressiveness that puts me on edge. Not to mention that I have had bad experiences with dogs of your breed in the past. I realize it's not fair to judge you by your appearance, but you can already sense my concerns and there is no need for me to try to disguise them."

"I will not harm you," came the response. Its softness did not match its sender. I wanted to say sarcastically, "Sure, right; I believe you," but I couldn't. The dog had integrity. Yet the mind chatter began again. What do you think you are doing? You must be crazy! Here you are in Iso thinking about taking Cujo outside. If this dog decides to turn on you, you're on your own. No one can hear you back here. I thought about going up front and just asking someone to listen out for me, but I knew they would try to talk me out of it. This dog was already labeled as vicious. Even though people at the shelter generally accepted my animal communication, they would not accept my putting others or myself at risk. I looked at the dog again. He picked up on my conflict and sent to me feelings of calmness. Finally I said, "Listen if I let you out and you bite or offer to bite me, that is it. No more help from me. If on the other hand you live up to your word, I will come back here daily to take you outside." He repeated, "I will not harm you."

With shaking hands I reached down to his furry body to place a leash on him. He stood perfectly still and I knew his stillness was to reassure me. As we walked down the aisle that separated the two rows of chain-link dog runs, he was slightly ahead of me. The other dogs in Iso barked frantically as we moved past their runs; the chow pranced by them with a strength and dignity. The pounding of my heart slowed and my hands steadied as we stepped outside. He sniffed the ground only briefly before choosing a location. Boy, he wasn't kidding when he said he had to relieve himself. After his "flood" of relief, I took him back into his run. He was a perfect gentleman. I thanked him and told him I'd be back. He had lived up to his word and now it was time for me to live up to mine.

Each day I would take him outside and soon a friendship developed. It took a while for the staff at the animal shelter to accept our friendship. But after a while they came to see him differently. They began to see that they had misinterpreted the "air" he carried about him. Most of the general public who entered the shelter could not see past his appearance and would label him mean or vicious, even though we never heard or saw him snap or growl at anyone. His name became Dusty, after his hair color.

I asked him about his background and he shared with me the information that he had once been someone's dog. Apparently his people had intended for him to protect a woodpile. He showed me an image of himself chained up in an inner-city area. The house he lived at appeared to be a one-story wooden house with green paint that was chipping. The steps leading to the front porch were crumbling concrete; the wooden porch bowed in the center. The houses on either side were not in much better condition. I saw no doghouse, just the disarrayed pile of scrap lumber and cut logs. A male person would feed him, reminding the dog that he needed to be "tough." Then the feedings became less frequent, along with any visits. People would pass by, giving him a wide berth. Anyone he started toward would either run or jump back further away from him. He disliked being chained, and finally one day he got loose. The people didn't seem to care. In fact they had decided he had grown too big and they were now frightened of him. He would roam the neighborhood, walking up on people's porches looking for food, only to be greeted by broomsticks and flying objects hurled at him. Weren't humans supposed to give him food? Why were they afraid of him? Even though he found human behavior frustrating, their abuse did not break his spirit. He was a survivor.

Dusty asked me about the fear he encountered from humans: "Why is this?" We were outside in our large grassy, fenced-in area and I was letting him run loose. Watching him run was like watching a wolf in the wild. He came alive outside. His eyes shone and his beautiful coat ruffled in the wind. His question reminded me of my first encounter with him. I realized that in essence he was a lone wolf. Some humans could never capture or understand his wild spirit. His independent nature and assuredness threatened most. I conveyed this thought to him. I told him that, sadly, most people were governed by first impressions and rarely looked deeper to see the total being or even why someone may appear a certain way. Why we humans had this tendency, I did not know.

What I do know is one day a dog who had been abandoned, beaten, and generally abused by humans was taken to an animal shelter. There he met a woman who was judging him just as the other humans had. She had put him in the category of vicious dogs. Yet he chose not to follow typical human behavior and make a judgment on what he saw on the outside. He looked deeper and saw the opportunity for something else. He reached out in trust and honesty and touched my heart forever.

After several months of searching for Dusty's new home, we found it. He moved to a farm where he was allowed to run free. I had some misgivings, but I knew that was the way he wanted it. So I honored his wish. In the end Dusty's freedom was the route to his ticket out of this lifetime. He was following his new person, who was driving a tractor across a road, when a car struck and killed my friend.

I was numb from the news. I went home and sat in the woods surrounding my property, the place I go to seek answers and solace. I felt a presence, just as I had the first time he introduced himself to me. I turned to look and there he stood. He was in spirit and yet real, as if he were there physically. He had come to let me know that he was okay and to tell me goodbye. "You are my friend," I heard. Then his image faded away.

THE NEED FOR RESPECT

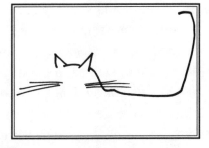

Working for the humane society was a conscious choice for me. I had decided it would be the perfect place to incorporate my animal communication abilities and improve my skill. Meanwhile I could do private consults and teach workshops on my days off. I knew of the emotional harm that the shelter had caused for others before me; just the same I was willing to take that risk. It became one of the most bittersweet experiences of my life, and definitely a place of powerful teachers and lessons.

Our front office at the humane society seemed like Grand Central Station most of the time. There was a long countertop that faced our reception window to the public. The counter was often cluttered with various forms, literature, and animal-related items such as leashes and collars. In one corner of the office stood a desk that was always covered with paperwork and had a constantly ringing phone. File cabinets, a copying machine, and two large stainless steel cages took up the rest of the wall space. Add to all of this six staff members coming and going, plus what we called the general public (visitors to the shelter), and you have Grand Central Station.

Early in my employ at the humane society, I happened to be in the front office looking through a file cabinet for a record when a man walked in holding a cat carrier. He was the type of man who would blend into a crowd easily: brown hair, glasses, average build and height. He seemed mildly uncomfortable. I saw Page, our office person, heading over to help him, so I continued on with my record search.

"Can I help you?" asked Page.

"Yes," he said, "I brought my cat to be euthanized."

There was no emotion in his voice, but he did shift his weight back and forth, expressing that discomfort I'd seen before in people who were dropping off animals.

"Can I ask why?" I'm not sure why Page formed it as a question; it was quite obvious that this was a polite demand. Page was a retired government employee who had a different style with the public. At first glance one might be deceived by this petite lady who loves animals; however, her patience ran thin in the face of ignorance in the care and well being of animals.

"Oh, well, all of a sudden she's taken to urinating on the carpets, not to mention she's been acting lethargic," said the man.

The aggravation in Page's voice gave hint that her temper matched her red hair.

"Have you taken her to the veterinarian to make sure there is no medical reason for her actions?"

"She's been checked and the doctor could not find any cause for her behavior. Look, we feel she is very unhappy and just doesn't wish to live anymore. So we want her put to sleep." The man had become defensive.

While he and Page were discussing the situation I peered into the carrier to see a beautiful, white, green-eyed cat. She huddled toward the back of the carrier, as if trying to get as far away from this conversation and place as possible. I didn't blame her.

Not able to keep my mouth shut anymore, I interrupted, saying, "Sir, this is a young beautiful cat. I wish you would just sign her over to us and give us a chance to find someone to adopt her. If the veterinarian found no problem with her health, that probably means she is unhappy about something in her present living conditions. Cats often urinate outside their litter boxes as a sign of protest or unhappiness. We may be able to find her a home that she would be better suited for, so she would not exhibit that behavior. Perhaps we won't, but at least it gives her a chance."

"Well, I can't imagine anyone wanting a cat like this," he remarked, "but she is actually my wife's cat, I suppose I could call her and run this past her."

Page handed him the phone and we just looked at each other. We both knew if he signed the request to put her to sleep, there was nothing we could legally do to stop him. It would be such a waste not to give this cat a chance. In so many similar cases, we had found appropriate homes for cats like this one.

"Okay," the man said after hanging up the phone, "my wife says we'll just sign her over for you to do as you deem necessary."

I quietly smiled to myself, "Yes!" I thought.

I took Jane (as I will call the cat) to a private holding room. The room was all concrete, with fluorescent lighting and no windows. At least it was quiet for the most part, for we usually housed only cats here. One side of the room was lined with stainless steel cages. Several of the cat occupants meowed a greeting to me.

Once inside I closed the door and proceeded to introduce the other cats to Jane. I then went on about how my intervention had bought Jane a second chance. Thinking back on it now, I have to laugh at my pompous self-righteousness in sounding like a person who thought she was a knight in shining armor. Not once had I stopped to ask Jane's opinion on things. I was too caught up in what a wonderful thing I had done for this cat. I prepared a cage for her, then went over and stooped down to unlock the door of her carrier.

"Come on sweetheart," I said as I reached in to pull out this poor, depressed cat. As my fingers came within inches of her, I heard, "Rawwll, hissss!" The cat came to life; with the fire of a tigress in her eyes she came at me.

The next thing I remembered was sitting on my backside with my foot holding the carrier door shut and Jane clawing at my shoe. She continued with a lower growl. The communication was clear, "Try it again lady. I'll show you who's helpless." Well so much for being the poor, pitiful little kitty. "Okay," I said, "you've gained my respect." I decided to give her a little time to cool down, not to mention time for me to regain my center.

Quite often cats would come into the shelter highly upset, acting aggressively, only to calm down in a day or two. Most cats hate relocation. They spend a lot of time balancing the energy in their homes the way they want it. I had hoped Jane would relax in time. Several days went by and Jane greeted every staff member with the same reception she gave me. Her attitude made caring for her less than pleasant, not to mention hazardous. Something had to be done, or I knew she would be a candidate for euthanasia.

I decided it was time to have a "talk" with Jane. Her cage was located on the bottom level so I had to crouch down for a proper view of her. I tuned in and asked, "Jane, what's the problem here?" I should have been better prepared. With the force of a strong shove her thoughts spit out at me: "People are stupid!"

"Okay," I thought, "guess I had that coming." I knew there was truth in what she was communicating. I replied, "You're right, many people are ignorant." Had this animal possessed a human face her jaw would have dropped. The thought came, "A human agreeing with me?" I let her digest this phenomenon. Suddenly there was a softening of her hard shell and I felt her pain and bitterness at being treated as a "stupid cat," whose feelings did not need to be considered.

"Jane, not all people are ignorant in that way. There are some who do respect animals. Look at me, sense my true nature. There are others like me. I would like to find you a new home in which you would have people who love and respect you. I can't put you up for adoption if you are going to attack everyone that you come in contact with. If you don't want me to help you find a home, then you will end up being sent to the spirit world. The choice is yours and I will honor it." It seemed like a long time before she replied, "I choose a new home with people who will respect me." I reminded her that this meant cooperation on her part. She communicated understanding.

Jane was never overly friendly, but after our conversation she did tolerate our care. Finally she had earned our trust and we were able to put her in the adoption room, where the general public could come to visit the cats. It was a bigger room, and even though its physical appearance was similar to the others, it had two open doors and a steady supply of visitors, which gave it a less isolated feel.

Shortly after being put in the adoption room, Jane received a visitor. "Hello, I'm Jane's owner," the woman said with strain in her voice. Her mousy brown hair was pulled back in a ponytail, and her face showed naivete.

"Is she still here?"

"Yes," I answered, wondering why this woman had come. It had been several weeks and we hadn't heard a peep from Jane's people.

"I just have to see her. I have been heartbroken since my husband brought her here."

I escorted her into the adoption room.

"Jane!" she squealed. "Oh, I've missed you so much. Are you okay, sweet little baby? I should have never sent you here. We missed having a cat so badly, we got a little kitten. . . ."

She was rambling on and on. I quickly understood how Jane had come to the conclusion that people were stupid. I tuned Jane's person out and tuned Jane in. The lady continued to ramble as I communicated with the cat. "Do you wish to go back to live with this person?" I asked.

"Are you kidding?" The reply came quickly.

"Okay, I will do my best to dissuade her."

How was I going to do this? Normally I am happy to reunite animals and their people. I enjoy helping them to resolve and/or work through difficulties. This time was different. It was obvious that Jane and this woman were not a match made in heaven. This woman could not give this cat the home she wanted or needed.

"Ma'am, excuse me, but I don't think it's a good idea to readopt Jane. She obviously was not happy there. As I had told your husband, cats usually don't urinate outside of their boxes without reason. Since she's been here I've come to know her pretty well. I think she'd do better in another home. One where she could get the attention she needs. I know you love her; however, I think if you took her home you'd be right back where you started. Please let me continue to look for another home for her."

The woman looked puzzled; I knew I was not convincing her. Jane was her cat and she knew what was best for her.

"Jane," I mentally communicated to the cat, "I need your help. She needs to know you don't want to go home with her." I wasn't sure what I wanted Jane to do or even if she would assist. I knew from my experience with this cat that she could get a message across quite well. It was up to her if she wished to stay and wait for another home. All of the sudden she stood up and turned around, presenting her backside to her former person. There she remained, not turning around once to look at this woman. She just stared at the back of her cage. Her body language did the trick.

"Aha, she doesn't seem to want anything to do with me." The disgruntled woman complained, a baffled look on her face. I didn't say a word. It was all I could do to keep from laughing. The woman made several attempts to get Jane's attention, but Jane's innate feline ability to ignore people won out. Finally the woman gave me an exasperated look.

"I think I can find Jane a home where she will be happy," I said in answer to her look.

"I guess you will have to." I felt her sadness, yet I knew it was ultimately for the best.

A week later, it was after lunch and I happened to walk into the cat adoption room to check on everyone. There on the floor sat a lady who frequented the humane society. She enjoyed coming by and visiting with the animals. I liked her a great deal, for she showed the animals not only love, but also a lot of respect. We'd come to know her well, and she had even adopted a few animals over the years. I leaned over to see who she was cuddling with today. There was Jane! She was kneading, purring, and yes, that was a smile I saw on her furry face! Jane had become somewhat affectionate with us, but I had never seen her warm up this much to anyone.

"I can't believe this!" I said. "That cat is normally very picky about who touches her, much less whose lap she sits in."

"Oh, really?" the lady replied. "She came right up to the cage and asked for me to get her out."

Jane looked up at me and in her face was softness, her eyes reflecting joy. I communicated, "You found your person, didn't you?"

"YES!"

Jane left that day for her new home.

THAT'S "MS." GOAT TO YOU

Be careful what you ask for. How many times have you heard that? For years I had commented on wanting a goat to come and live with me. I never really acted upon it because my husband wasn't as excited about it as I was. One day, toward the end of my employment at the humane society, an animal warden came into the shelter.

"Patty!" he yelled.

I came running, thinking something was wrong. "What . . . ." My voice trailed off as my eyes fell upon a small white and gray goat. She looked up at me through bashful eyes.

"Oh my. . .where did you find her?" On her neck was a leather collar to which the warden had attached a dog leash. She was pulling hard on the leash as he tried to show her to me. She managed to keep her body behind the man, but her little head peeked out around his pants leg.

"Got a call that she was wandering loose in the city limits. You said you wanted a goat. She's a nanny goat too." He smiled. "Although I expect whoever she belonged to will be looking for her. She had that collar on when I picked her up."

She was adorable. She wore a childlike look on her face, and her button horns indicated she was indeed young. I couldn't resist anymore and reached down to stroke her head. She pulled away, looking at me suspiciously.

"That's okay, sweetheart. I know this is a strange place with strange people."

I knew the warden was right. Her people would probably come after her, but until then she needed someone to care for her. I took her to an empty dog run and escorted her inside. I began to communicate to her. "This is really going to seem strange. I doubt you are used to hard, smooth floors and noisy dogs. I apologize, but this was the only safe place to put you. I promise you that you are safe."

I waited for some sort of reply. I got nothing except that feeling of suspicion again. "This is understandable," I thought.

Suspicion was not good, yet I was glad to know that she was not terrified or frightened.

I took on caring for the goat as my personal responsibility. I enjoyed feeding her and, when I had the time, I'd take her outside to graze in the yard. I took care not to become emotionally attached, thinking her people would be coming in any day to reclaim her. She did her part in keeping the distance between us. Each day I'd talk with her. I would like to say I was communicating, but communication usually requires two parties and she wasn't participating. It became clear to me that I was dealing with a prejudiced goat. The suspicion I had sensed was mixed with disdain toward me, this strange human. It was a bit frustrating, but I knew how important it was to allow her space and to respect her wishes.

Several days passed and no one inquired about the goat. I started calling her "Ms. Goat," not knowing what her name was or what she might like to be called. Normally I let my animal friends pick their names, but "Miss Friendly" wasn't helpful on this account either.

The humane society is legally bound to hold any stray animal for a certain number of days before that animal is put up for adoption. This is to allow the animal's people an opportunity to come in and "reclaim" the animal. Ms. Goat's holding time passed without a single inquiry, to my husband's disappointment.

So I told Ms. Goat all about her new home—her home with me. I visualized the rock-clad landscape and the rolling hills and woods surrounding our home. Then I visualized the other animals that lived there. Visualization is very important in my communications. Showing this little goat where she was going would give her an idea what to expect; I hoped it would make the transition into her new home easier.

"I do not expect you to be a pet," I said. "I just want to give you a good and loving home. If you do not wish to be stroked and cuddled, that is fine. I only ask that you allow me to touch you when necessary." Still I received a feeling of suspicion. "Lord, you are a tough one," I said. "Just don't want to let me in, huh?"

When she arrived at our home, the other animals were all prepared. I had taken the time to let them know of the addition to our family. They were all anxious to see this goat. I was not surprised at the acceptance my animals showed her, for they have typically been good sports about newcomers. What did surprise me was how quickly she took to them. Actually I was a little insulted. I had been respectful and not once pushy in my interactions with her, yet I continued to be snubbed.

After she moved in with us she had begun to answer my questions, although she communicated with me as little as possible. She was keeping distance between us. On a walk one day I decided to ask her what she wanted her name to be. She trotted off ahead as if she was going to ignore me. Then, with a lift of her chin and a feeling of irritation toward this annoying human, she communicated, "Ms. Goat will do." This was typical of our interactions, short and sweet. What did I have to do to get this goat's acceptance? The answer came quickly from within. You must continue to allow her to be. You cannot make her respect or trust you. She has the right to choose with whom she interacts, just as you do.

A few weeks passed, during which I made peace with my relationship with Ms. Goat. The door to my heart remained open in case she wished to enter. I no longer held expectations. I had decided to invite another dog into our home. It was Dusty the chow chow. I was leaving the humane society soon and still hadn't found a home for him. I had communicated to him as I had to Ms. Goat, what my home and the animals living there were like. Sadly, the feeling I got from him when I mentioned Ms. Goat was one of intense interest. He was intensely interested in eating her, that is. I loved Dusty so much that I thought perhaps we could work this out; perhaps I could get him to change his mind about Ms. Goat's purpose. I had to try, I thought, so I took him home.

As we got out of the car I put Dusty on a leash. The dogs came out to meet him, and after their traditional dog introductions—tail sniffing and so forth—all was fine. Suddenly Dusty lost interest in the dogs. He was staring off toward the fenced-in area. There stood Ms. Goat, wide-eyed with curiosity. Her innocence toward other animals was amazing. "Hi!" came the greeting from goat to dog. From Dusty I felt a primal reaction. There was no acknowledgment that this goat was trying to welcome him. He saw only a potential meal. I tried to communicate with him and he shut me out. I took him out of her sight and again communicated that Ms. Goat was part of the family, not prey. He communicated back that he was unwilling to change his mindset. "Do you understand that you cannot live with me if you cannot live in harmony with Ms. Goat?" I said. "Yes," came the answer. He loved me, but she would always be prey in his eyes, and he was unwilling to compromise.

I was heartbroken and angry at Dusty at the same time. The anger didn't last long, as I came to terms with the fact that he had made his position clear before I had even brought him here. What did I expect? I thought to myself. I knew inside it had been an act of desperation. I was afraid Dusty would not find a home. I couldn't bear that thought. I started considering finding Ms. Goat another home. After all, she was cute and young and I knew of several people who would love to have her live with them. Hey, wait a minute, this was Ms. Goat's home before it was Dusty's, I reminded myself. Ms. Goat had made it clear that she loved the other animals. I had no right to send her away.

It seemed as if the Universe was playing a cruel joke on me. Here was Dusty who loved me, and I loved him, yet we couldn't live together because of another animal who acted as if she couldn't care less about me. Inside I knew that Dusty was not meant to live with me, and he knew it too. He knew that he had crossed my path to serve a purpose. He had come to remind me of the need for honesty and the need to trust my communication abilities, and to remind me not to judge a book by its cover. That purpose being complete, he would move on. The animals amaze me with their ability to move forward. I could not conceal my anguish as I put Dusty into my car and drove him back to the humane society.

When I returned home that evening I went to feed Ms. Goat. As I bent over to pick up her metal bowl, I started crying again. I closed my eyes, trying to stop the tears. Ever so softly I felt a nuzzle on my cheek and I could feel her soft breath as she sniffed around my eyes. I opened my eyes and she communicated an understanding that I had made a sacrifice for her. Then in an effort to comfort me she said, "I do like it here." That day, Ms. Goat walked through the open door of my heart.

Since then she has shown us that her role in our household is to entertain. Before her barn was built we allowed her to stay with our dogs. They have a dog door to the basement so that, should the weather get bad, they can go in and out of the basement at will. When I return home, if the dogs are not already outside they run out the dog door to greet me.

One particular afternoon I thought it was odd that no one emerged. I hurried into the house and headed down the basement stairs to see what was up. I got halfway down the steps when I saw them. "What on earth?!" I said aloud. I could not believe my eyes. There, lodged in the dog door, were Mauvree, my oldest female black Lab, and Ms. Goat. On Ms. Goat's head was a turban, made of a large striped rug. The "turban" wrapped around her horns and draped across her back, ending somewhere outside. Pethee, my youngest black Lab, and C.C., my male yellow, were standing inside cheering Mauvree and Ms. Goat as they attempted to dislodge themselves from the entrapment of the door. If it weren't for the desperation in Mauvree's eyes I would have run upstairs for my camera. As it was, Mauvree was pleading with me for help. She was easily freed, but Ms. Goat's turban restricted her movement, as the end of it was caught in the dog door. I released the free-flowing turban and went to help Ms. Goat remove it from her horns. She wasn't quite ready to give up her new fashion design and pranced around the basement with half the rug flapping behind her. Pethee, my eternal puppy, decided this was meant to be a game of tug-of-war and grabbed the loose part of the turban. My laughter only added to the sense that this was a fun sport. With Ms. Goat wailing as Pethee pulled on her turban, I had to compose myself and communicate to Pethee and Ms. Goat that this was not a game. To Pethee's disappointment I cut Ms. Goat's entangled attire off her horns.

Ms. Goat loved dog biscuits. My husband Joe went downstairs one day to give her and each of the dogs a biscuit. "Patty, get down here quick," he shouted up to me. I dropped what I was doing, fearing that he had found someone injured.

"What's going on?" I shouted back as I hurried toward the stairs.

"You're not going to believe this," he answered.

I arrived at the bottom of the steps to see a Milk-Bone box with a goat body and legs. Somehow she had gotten her entire head inside of the biscuit box. After consuming all of the biscuits she had decided to check for any crumbs in the bottom of the box. Now the box was where her head should have been.

"You look ridiculous," I communicated.

"So what? They were delicious," she communicated back as she smacked her lips with satisfaction.

DEFINITION OF FRIENDSHIP

One of the most touching aspects to my communication work is the love that I feel and experience between animals and their human companions. I have received a greater understanding of love through animal communication work than through any other experience life has given me. Animal communication goes beyond the verbal, and it is sometimes difficult to express what I receive with words.

A friend asked me to communicate with her dog, Rosie, whom she'd met at the local S.P.C.A. Rosie, who was of a mixed spaniel heritage, was a petite, tri-colored dog with long, flowing hair and a curly tail. "She had the sweetest face and the saddest eyes," recalled my friend, Becky. "She tugged at my heartstrings so I took her out for a walk. The whole time I visited her at the shelter she kept her tail between her legs. I had to adopt her. Once we got home, within an hour the tail shot up in the air, and from that point on she was always having a good time."

Clairabelle the beagle was already living with Becky before Rosie moved in. Becky would take Clairabelle and Rosie with her as much as possible. For many small dogs, looking out the window of a car presents a problem. But Rosie did not want to miss out on anything. Looking out the window is a must for a dog like Rosie. She decided she could overcome her height challenges. Clairabelle became the perfect booster seat, providing her with enough elevation so that her front feet could comfortably reach the armrest and give her the ultimate front-seat view. According to Becky, Clairabelle was a good sport about it. "Rosie was sent to me because Clairabelle was getting ready to leave me," Becky added. "About a month after Rosie moved in, Clairabelle died of renal failure. Rosie helped me through Clairabelle's death."

Becky went on to tell me of all the joy Rosie brought into her life as well as other people's. "Everybody loved Rosie. She brought smiles to everyone's face. My sister, who up to that point was not a dog person, cared for Rosie while I was out of the country for two months. Rosie made such an impression that my sister now has a dog who looks a lot like my Rosie." Becky's face lit up with fondness as she shared her memories of this dear friend, and I thought to myself, "Rosie still brings you joy."

The connection that remained was what brought Becky to ask about her Rosie, who now had passed on into the spirit world. When I tuned into Rosie she told me she had something to share about friendship. She told me that this message reflected all those in the animal kingdom who chose to have relationships with humans. For me it has become the definition of friendship, as given by a master on the subject.

"Many do not know the definition of friendship. Friendship goes beyond color, size, gender, or even species. A friend loves no matter what. There are times when friends may not approve of each other's behavior, and friends occasionally have opposing views, but they still love and respect each other. A friend is loyal and allows freedom to be. A friend is there in times of need, supporting. Friendship provides a safe place, and yet sometimes a friend asks us to stretch. We grow and flourish in the company of a friend. Friends see us for who we truly are, equal partners in this journey.

"You came to me when I was in need. You gave the freedom to be. You saw in me a being worthy of respect and

dignity. In your company I flourished. You allowed me to be and yet invited me to grow. I knew your love was genuine, without conditions. I enjoyed my dog friends, but you were the love of my life...."

—Rosie, a dog, through Patty Summers

JULIO'S MESSAGE

I couldn't believe it when Debbie pointed him out to me. "Look Patty, I love him." Before me stood a matted mass of black hair. He reminded me of an old filthy dust mop. He was ten years old, blind, deaf, and grouchy. This really wasn't surprising to me; Debbie was always falling in love with the hard-luck cases. It was rather obvious why the miniature poodle had been surrendered to the humane society. He had become a burden to his humans, a sad, frequent occurrence. Debbie filled out the paperwork and in minutes he had a new home. There he acquired a reputation for being a feisty little guy. Nothing was off limits according to his rules. Debbie referred to him as her "cranky old man." He was a challenging dog, set in his ways of doing things, yet one thing was clear: he adored Debbie and she him. He had been living with Debbie two years when I resigned from the humane society to go to work at a veterinary hospital.

I was in the back setting up for a surgery scheduled for that day. I was carrying the stainless steel instruments the doctor would need into the surgery room when the receptionist called me to the phone.

"Hello?" I said.

An anxious voice answered, "Patty, it's Julio. He's dying; I just know it." It was Debbie. She began sobbing. "Can the doctor see him?"

"Of course," I said.

I was unaware of her arrival, due to the fact that I was assisting one of the doctors at the time. We had two veterinarians, so the one who was available rushed in to help Julio. A while later, I turned to see Dr. John walking down the hallway toward me. He had a serious look on his face as he said in a soft voice, "Patty, your friend is here. She wants to see you. The little dog is in heart failure and there isn't anything I can do to save him. She has decided to have me put him to sleep."

Numbly I walked to the exam door and stood there a minute. I tried to prepare myself for the scene I was about to encounter. Slowly I opened the door. Across the room Julio lay on the stainless steel examination table. His eyes were glazed over and there was blood mixed with saliva from where he had vomited. His little body rose and fell with labored breathing. Debbie was cradling him in her arms, rocking him back and forth, her face streaked with tears. "It's okay baby, I love you," she said between sniffles. It was tender and heartbreaking. The love that a human feels for an animal is so strongly expressed in times like these.

I gave her a comforting hug. "I'm sorry," I said. There was nothing else I could say at the time. I had to let her feel her pain. "Pain is a part of life," a dog once told me. "Pain is not something to run from. It is simply part of the experience. It is not bad; it just is."

As I stood there offering a shoulder for my friend, I felt a familiar request. A tuning in from the animal, who wanted to communicate something to me. I knew Julio had something to share. I could not clearly tune into him in such an emotional atmosphere, so as soon as it was appropriate I left the room. Julio was insistent that I give his person a message from him. Even while dying, Julio was impatient about having his requests honored. I found some quiet time and tuned into his message:

"When my people took me to that place, I felt my worthiness was gone. I was a throwaway. My body was worn

out and I was no longer considered a showpiece to my people. All my life I was appreciated for my physical appearance and I had grown to believe that my physical appearance was all I had. Since I no longer had worth, I had decided that I was brought to this place to die. Then you saw me, but you weren't really looking at my body. You were looking beyond. I realized you were looking at the real me, the one inside that I had forgotten existed. You awakened a part of me that had been dormant for some time. I then knew that I had been taken to this place not to die, but to remember what life is really all about: LOVE.

"The time we had together was the best time of my life. It made time on Earth worth it. I hope you will find that what you are looking for is already within yourself. . . . Love is the most important thing in life. . . ."

—Julio, a dog, through Patty Summers

TOSSING MY HEAD
INTO THE WIND

I had arrived at the farm for an appointment and pulled into the fence-lined driveway that ran alongside the field in which the horses were kept. Sandy, the lady with whom I had the appointment, was right; it was a beautiful farm. Nestled in the Blue Ridge Mountains, the gentle rolling fields were bordered by woods on one side and a gravel road on the other. No other homes were in sight, which added to the farm's peaceful solitude.

As I got out of my car, I took notice of the five horses and the pony that had stopped grazing to look up at me. I could feel their curiosity. The white mare and chestnut pony only watched me briefly before going back to enjoying the sweet grass. The three geldings showed more interest. It was the dirty white one that caught my eye. He had been rolling in some mud, so his white coat had a reddish tint to it. Looks like he's had some fun, I thought. Slowly and deliberately he left the herd and approached the fence. He walked with confidence, his eyes meeting mine. His body language made it clear that he had something to say.

"Are you the person that has come to communicate with us?" Apparently his person, Sandy, had taken the time to let them know about my visit. "Yes," I replied. I was glad to know that Sandy had communication with her animals. He raised his head just a bit and stated, "I'm the King horse." I acknowledged him. I felt his assuredness was not egotism, but confidence in his role and position in his herd. I excused myself, promising to return. Right now I needed to meet his person. This was agreeable to him, so I proceeded to the house.

I felt from meeting Comet that I would also enjoy meeting Comet's person, and I did. She not only loved her animals, she respected them. Sandy had long, graying dark hair that she kept braided in a ponytail. She had clear blue eyes and she wore no makeup. There was a natural beauty about her. She shared her farm with Muffin the pig, who adored her rabbit companion,

Costishino; there were dogs, Echo the cat, goldfish, birds, and of course the horses. When I told Sandy that Comet had introduced himself to me as the King, she was not surprised. "Comet is my oldest horse and yes, he is the boss horse among the others."

Sandy and Comet's relationship began when Comet was a colt. His former people orphaned Comet, on purpose, due to the accidental breeding of his horse mother. Because they considered Comet a mistake and a burden, they gave him to the local veterinarian. The veterinarian decided he didn't have time for the colt. So plans were made to ship him away, in order to be killed for pet food. As fate would have it, Sandy's cousin had been friends with the veterinarian's son, and the cousin intervened. Comet went to live on her cousin's farm and it was there that Sandy grew to know him. "I loved this horse from the moment I met him," she told me.

Sandy asked to make Comet "officially" her horse by the time he was a yearling. For twenty-six years they lived together. They shared much. He saw Sandy through many life changes such as jobs, marriage and divorce, remarriage, and the birth of Sandy's daughter Jackie. Sandy told me that running was a passion of hers and that she satisfied that passion through running track in school. Now when she ran, Comet would often run beside her. Sandy was an artist and had even named her company after her friend Comet, calling it "Comet Strips." He was a very important part of her life.

A little over a year after my first introduction to Sandy, Comet, and the rest of the family, they moved to a new location. They had been at their new farm about a month when I received a desperate phone call.

"Patty this is Sandy, I need your help. I found Comet down this morning. I've called the veterinarian and she is on her way, but I want you to check in with him and find out what happened."

She had found Comet in a wooded area of the property. He was lying down with a distant look on his face, as if his body was here, but his spirit was not. The only indication that he was alive was his shallow breathing. When she called out his name he lifted his head slightly. Through a lot of encouragement she somehow got him to his feet. By the time Sandy had called me, she had managed to get him alert enough to stand and walk back to the barn.

Comet still felt dazed to me during the communication with him; however, he was able to give me a visual picture of what had happened. I saw a group of dogs: one black, probably a Lab mix, a large dark brown dog that resembled a German shepherd, and several hound-like dogs with short hair, floppy ears, and black, white, and brown markings. The dogs were full of themselves; they reminded me of a group of people who had just stepped out of a bar, drunk and obnoxious. They were out looking for a "fun time." Comet was chased into the woods, where the dogs circled him, barking and nipping at his legs. Even though the dogs did not physically touch him, the terror was enough to put a horse of his age into shock.

The dogs were allowed to roam the neighborhood at will and were offered very little companionship from their people. Like people, many dogs need some form of mental stimulation or sense of purpose. Dogs came to be our companions, and it is natural for them to seek out human companionship. When this is withheld or given only in minuscule amounts, the dog tends to seek outside stimulation or the company of other dogs. The company of other dogs wouldn't be so bad except that, just like people, dogs can be affected by a group's energy. If one of the group acts on his or her instinct to hunt, the others are likely to follow suit. They get caught up in the moment. If these dogs were a true part of their human family, it probably could have been avoided.

I asked Comet to hang in there. He was safe now and I communicated calmness. Sandy told me that if Comet felt he could not go on, she could let him go, but she would do whatever she could if he wished to live. She loved and respected her friend and was willing to abide by his wishes, as painful as that might be. Comet was too much in shock to make any decision at that time. I explained that the best thing we could do for him right now was help him ground or collect himself. When I ended the consult, I felt he was shaky, yet mentally "present." I finished up by reminding him of Sandy's willingness to do what he wished. The veterinarian arrived to confirm that he was in shock. She did what she could for him medically and told Sandy the rest was up to Comet.

Early the next morning I awoke to sadness. I felt the horse had passed on to the spirit world. My feeling was confirmed by a telephone call from Sandy.

"I'm not doing very well, my King is dead."

I felt the terrible emptiness in her heart. "I'm sorry for your pain," I said. "Take your time to grieve, but I hope you find some peace in knowing that only the physical body is dead. His spirit lives on."

"Thank you," she replied.

It was several days later when I was outside and I heard a familiar "voice." I stopped what I was doing and focused in. It was Comet. He wished to share with me a message for Sandy. I was thrilled to receive it. It came to me as follows.

"Tossing my head into the wind, I was the King and you are my friend. I came to share the spirit of my being (the spirit

of the horse). Even though others did not recognize my power and who I truly was, I did. I knew my destiny, my path. So it was no surprise when you brought me into your life. We were meant to journey together. I shared with you the power of the horse. The power of freedom to be who you are, no matter what another suggests. The power to know your worth and the glorious power of a loving friendship. I carried you through personal challenges and loneliness. Together we ran in an expression of joy and exhilaration. We shared much, love, laughter, and tears, all expressions of life. You and I are a part of one another. As I run with strength and dignity I carry you, my friend, with me. I still share my medicine with you and this shall always be so. Hold me in your heart, dear friend, and know that you are always carried in mine. When you are weary I will still carry you, when you are joyous, I will be running beside you; when you need to stop to contemplate, I will wait for you. I continue to journey with you."

—Comet, a horse, through Patty Summers

QUEEN
HONEY BOO

I was working at an animal hospital when the receptionist came back to the treatment area where I normally worked and said, "Patty, I'm going to have my sister bring her cat over for the doctors to take a look at."

April was a young woman in her early twenties. Her sensitivity toward the clients made her an asset to the hospital. Her concern was written all over her face as she continued, "Something is really wrong. The cat has lost some of her hair, is losing a lot of weight, and seems depressed."

"I'm sorry to hear this," I said. "Hope it turns out to be nothing serious."

"Me too. Honey Boo lived with us when we were growing up. When my sister got married, Honey Boo went with her. My sister really loves Honey Boo, but this comes at a really bad time, since my sister is due to have her baby in less than a month."

"That's right," I replied. "I forgot she was pregnant." The phone rang so April went back up to the reception area to answer it.

It was later that morning when I saw April and her sister walking into the treatment area. In the sister's arms was what appeared to be an old, white, short-haired cat. Her face looked drawn and her eyes were tired. Dr. Sharon was with me when they walked in.

"This is Honey Boo," April said. "Do you have time to take a look at her now?"

"Sure," the doctor answered. "Patty, please go weigh her and get her temperature while I finish writing out some notes from the previous client."

As I picked up the frail-looking cat, I looked deeper into her eyes. Sadness and an immense feeling of hopelessness filled me. I placed her on the baby scale that we often used to weigh cats. She did not struggle, just sat there in the curved plastic tray gazing off into the distance. Five pounds. Wow, that's pretty light for a cat with this body size. I took Honey Boo's temperature and returned to Dr. Sharon, April, and her sister.

"How old is Honey Boo?" I asked.

"She's close to eight years."

I was shocked. I expected her to say she was at least 13 or 14. I had two cats in my family that were older than her and looked much younger. I put Honey Boo on the stainless steel examining table and Dr. Sharon's gentle hands began to examine her.

Afterwards the doctor said to April's sister, "I think we need to run some blood work on Honey Boo. Although her temperature is fine, her weight is unusually low, and her coat is in poor shape."

"Of course," replied the attractive and very pregnant woman. "Do you have any idea what's going on?"

"I don't want to speculate at this time. The blood work should give me the answers I need. Why don't you leave her here, we'll draw some blood and send it out to the lab right away. I'll have the results this afternoon."

Dee, Honey Boo's person, stroked Honey a few times and said her goodbyes.

"I'll call you as soon as I know something," Dr. Sharon said.

"I'll be here to keep an eye on her," April added. This seemed to give Dee some comfort.

The phone call April had been waiting for finally came. As soon as she finished copying the information down, she rushed it back to the doctor. Dr. Sharon studied the information as April anxiously stood by. When the vet looked up, she had a puzzled look on her face.

"Well I've got good news," she said. "Her blood work came back with all her functions at normal levels. Which is great since I had suspicions toward cancer. There are a few more tests we can run, but my feeling now is that the problem is psychological. We'll need to call your sister and find out how she wants us to proceed; meanwhile I'd like Patty to communicate with Honey Boo."

April agreed, and she called her sister while I went to "talk" with Honey Boo.

I approached the holding cage. Honey Boo was laying on a blue towel April had put inside for her comfort. I met the dullness in her eyes and felt her depression.

"What causes you to feel this way?" I mentally asked. She sent me visual images of her sitting on a high post bed. She looked stately and felt proud. Then she showed me Dee, her person. She was talking softly and adoringly to Honey Boo. She accepted her loving soft strokes. Honey Boo said she felt like a Queen.

Suddenly the image faded and a man appeared. He was tall with dark hair and he showed little interest in Honey Boo. His attention was solely directed to Dee. Dee directed a fair amount of her attention to this man as well. I knew this was Dee's husband. The thought came, "This was bad enough, but when this came (an image of a large black Lab came barreling into the picture), I'd had enough. I cannot live under these conditions." Honey Boo felt the dog was a slobbering, clumsy being. "Why did they have affection for this dog?" She wanted the attention to be focused on her, as it had been before. I acknowledged the cat and told her I'd relay her feelings to Dee.

Later that evening when Dee stopped in, I told her of my conversation with Honey Boo.

"Yes, Honey Boo was the center of my attention for many years. I have spoiled her. My life has changed now, though, and she needs to adapt to that."

"Well, I have met other animals like Honey, and to tell them to adapt won't work," I answered. "Honey is what I call a 'Queen Cat.' She is a more dignified, stately being, who expects to be treated with respect. To not get the respect or dignity that she feels she needs will either anger her or cause her to slip into a depressive state. Honey Boo no longer feels important to you."

"I do still love her and she is important to me; it's just that my life is different and I have other priorities," Dee said.

"There are things you can do to let her know she is still wonderful and that she has her unique position in the household. Is there any way that Honey could have a room that the dog wasn't allowed to go into, such as your bedroom?"

"No that wouldn't be fair to the dog."

"Okay what about Honey getting some quality time with just you? I'm not talking about hours; it could be ten minutes each day that you can give her your full attention. Talking with her and perhaps grooming or petting her?"

"With my work schedule and the baby coming, I'm not sure what things are going to be like in the future. I really don't feel like I'm going to be able to give Honey Boo what she wants."

"Well then," I replied, "I recommend we offer her the option of a new home where she can be a 'Queen' again."

Dee looked at Honey Boo and sighed. "Ask her if that is what she wants."

Dr. Sharon, who was standing in the room during the conversation, spoke up. "Perhaps Honey Boo could live here at the hospital and be our Queen Kitty. Would you feel okay about that, Dee?"

"I want her to be happy. It makes me sad to see her looking like this and being so depressed. At least if she lived here I'd know she was being taken good care of."

"Okay, I'll tell her the options," I said.

I focused on Honey Boo and told her that her person's life had changed, yet she did still love her. "Dee understands your needs and due to her life changes she feels she cannot give you the lifestyle or relationship you used to have with her." I showed Honey a mental picture of Dee having a baby. Honey said she was aware of this coming as well. She felt sad because she knew the baby was the final addition that would forever alter Dee's affections toward her. Honey had decided the relationship was over, so she might as well die. "Honey Boo, your life with Dee has changed forever and I understand that this causes you sadness. Have you thought of sharing with another human? Dr. Sharon said this animal hospital could use a Queen such as yourself and would like to know if you'd like the position." I began visualizing to her an image of her sitting regally on a fluffy towel watching the different activities at the hospital with staff members treating her with respect. She was intrigued, and decided to give it a chance.

From that day forward, Honey Boo was known as Queen Honey Boo. It didn't take long before she interacted with us and showed interest in her new role. Her appetite returned along with some weight. Soon her pretty white fur thickened, to affirm that Honey Boo was feeling much better. She was treated as part of the staff, and part of the staff she was. We all loved her and she especially had captured the heart of our youngest staff member, Mesha. Mesha was very connected to Honey Boo and read her well.

One day Honey had jumped out of her cage and hopped into another animal's bed that was lying on the floor. She then proceeded to make eye contact with Mesha, telling her, "I want one of these." Mesha took the hint, and we bought a new bed (or "throne," as we referred to it). During the day we would allow Honey to dwell in our conference room, always making sure her throne was where she was. In the evenings we would place the Queen in her throne and usually the "Carrier of the Queen" would make a processional out of returning her to her evening living quarters. Honey Boo loved it.

All was going well until the day two beautiful Maine coon cats came to board. The cage in which we chose to house them was directly under Honey Boo's. These handsome guys had personalities to match their physical appearances. We were quite taken by them and consequently gave them a great deal of our attention. Shortly after they arrived, we began to notice a certain Queen Kitty was becoming a little hostile when we went to care for her. One staff member suffered a pretty good scratch. Honey Boo might as well have had a can of green paint poured on her, for her envy was that obvious. I reassured Honey Boo that she was still the Queen, yet it seemed to have little effect in appeasing her.

I was heading out the door the evening after the staff member got scratched when Dr. John stopped me.

"Patty," he asked, "I take it Honey Boo is jealous of the new boarders?"

"You guessed it," I answered. "I told her she was still the Queen, but it didn't do any good. She's still angry."

"I see," he said as he stared off as if in contemplation.

I waited a moment to see if he had something to add, but apparently he was deep in thought. "See ya tomorrow morning," I said as I left.

The next morning was very busy. Between checking in new clients and caring for the animals that were already at the hospital, I had my work cut out for me. The early-morning routine seemed to fly by. Before I knew it, the vets had arrived. Dr. Sharon went into a treatment room to see a client, and Dr. John came back to go over the records of the animals that had been dropped off that day for surgery or treatment.

"How's our Queen today, Patty?"

I paused and reviewed my morning. Yes, come to think of it she had seemed more relaxed this morning. "You know, she seemed more like herself this morning. She even asked to be stroked and she hasn't done that in a few days."

"Good," he said.

I gave him a questioning look.

"I had a talk with Honey Boo last night after you left. Told her that each of us had a job to perform at this hospital and that it was the staff's job to make the other animals more comfortable while they were in our care. As Queen, her job was to be a hostess and to make the other animals, her guests, feel welcome. I asked her as Queen to help the other animals to feel safe in the hospital as well. Wasn't sure if she got it," he added grinning, "but I felt like she did."

I smiled back. How cool, I thought, a veterinarian making the effort to connect with his feline staff member. I turned to Honey Boo, who was sitting near us during this conversation. There was gratitude at the recognition this man had shown. Grace and dignity flowed from her being. Her self-esteem was strong and healthy like the body she now had.

Shortly after I left the hospital to pursue full-time work as an animal communicator, Mesha had me ask Honey Boo if she'd like to reign at her home. She'd talked it over with her mom, who had agreed. Honey Boo was delighted at the prospect of living with her friend. There she rules with an iron paw and a happy heart. Long live the Queen. . .Honey Boo.

GIFT OF GRACE

We tried so hard to give the puppies a chance. It seemed they came to us facing impossible odds. The man who brought the pups to the humane society said he had found the mother dog shot dead and the three pups with their eyes still closed, huddled close to her lifeless body. I was concerned for their survival at such a young age. My immediate concerns turned out to be unfounded, as they seemed to flourish. Time flew by, and at seven weeks old, they were eating on their own and ready to be adopted.

There was a great deal of interest in the pups, and the first day they went up for adoption one of them got a home. Several days later a staff member noticed the diarrhea in the kennel where we kept the remaining two pups. I asked Page to call the people who had adopted the puppy the previous day and have them take the pup to the veterinarian. Then I took the remaining pups to a quarantine area. I had just gotten the pups settled in when Mandy, another staff member, walked up to me.

"Patty," she said, her voice soft and weary, "Page said the adopters had just taken the pup to the vet this morning." She paused and swallowed. "The puppy died of parvo shortly after getting there."

"Damn," I muttered. I looked at the two Lab mixes. Their sweet brown eyes were full of innocence and they wagged their tails weakly as if to apologize for getting sick.

Mandy reached into their cage and stroked their soft, cream-colored fur. "They are so sweet," she said. "Poor babies, I'm sorry," she added. Parvo is a disease that attacks the intestines. It is quite often fatal in pups and highly contagious. Once symptoms such as diarrhea with blood are visible, the disease has already progressed far enough that saving a puppy's life is unlikely. The shelter's stance on parvo was euthanasia. Our manager was off that day, so it became my sad duty to euthanize the pups.

"I am sorry," I communicated to them. "We did our best. I guess it wasn't good enough to keep you from getting sick. You are going to a wonderful place." I then visualized the spirit world to the best of my ability. They communicated understanding and peace toward what was about to occur.

Animals have taught me much about death. Most importantly that death is nothing to be feared. It is a natural stage. The physical body is the means to experience life on Earth. Once that experience is over, the body is no longer needed. The being, however, continues on. How many times have we heard this in one way or another? If we believe this, why do we still fear death? The animals believe this because they KNOW it to be so. Like us, they have survival instincts and, unlike us, they do not fear death.

Mandy cradled each pup in her arms as I gave the lethal injection. They peacefully left their bodies and entered the spirit world. Even though I knew the pups were starting on the next phase of their journeys, I still had a heavy heart, due not to their deaths, but to the circumstances of their deaths. When Mandy left the room I remained, to be alone and deal with my feelings. As my tears flowed so did my anger, frustration, and pain.

Why? This is not fair. Why am I working in this place? What kind of person am I that I can put puppies to sleep? Oh, God I hate myself and what this place puts me through. I continued to sob a moment more when I felt her presence. I focused my swollen eyes on a carrier, and inside sat what most people would refer to as an alley cat. She was a gray and black tabby, slender, with rather large ears and eyes.

"What are you doing here?" I questioned. "Oh no, you were in here watching me put those pups to sleep, weren't you? Oh. . . ." I was filling up with self-loathing. "You must hate me," I communicated.

To my astonishment I heard a beautiful feminine voice. "Do not weep. We do not hate you or hold animosity toward you. We love you," came the voice. A feeling of love that verbal language cannot describe surrounded me. I closed my eyes and basked in this wonderful, healing love. She continued, "We understand what you do. The only judgments placed are by you. Your intentions and heart are true. There are times that will seem unfair or difficult. Operate from your heart and know all is well." A simple thank-you seemed trite, yet I was too busy digesting what she'd shared to come up with anything else. Later that day I inquired about the cat to find she was a stray who had contracted upper respiratory disease (a cold) and was supposed to be in the treatment area.

Several weeks later Page was severely bitten by another cat. The bite was so severe that a doctor had to treat her. When she returned I approached her.

"How are you doing?" I asked.

She pulled back her bandage to expose her red, inflamed wrist with two nasty puncture wounds.

"Well, I'll survive," she joked, "however, her teeth did go all the way to my bone, and I'll be on antibiotics for a while. You know, I have to share with you what happened after the bite. You will probably be the only one who will believe it," she lowered her head, shook it and laughed. "I swear to you that a tabby cat in the same room said to me, 'I'm sorry that one of my species would have harmed you.' I was dumbfounded."

"What?" I said. "Page, could you show me the cat that said this to you?"

We walked into the room and before Page could point her out, I knew who it was. There she sat, "Miss Alley Cat." She blinked and looked at me. I once again met the wisdom in her eyes.

That evening I went home and told my husband Joe about Page and the cat. I had told him about what had happened to me before. "I get the feeling she is supposed to live with us," I said.

"Patty, we already have four cats. . . ." He stopped as he looked into my eyes and knew there was no need to remind me of this. "Just make sure you clear it with the other cats first," he said in resignation.

"Already have," I replied cheerfully.

Shortly thereafter, Kallee moved in. My husband had suggested the name to her and she had agreed to it. Kallee means "good" or "well" in Greek. We thought it fit, as she had been a good friend to me and had spread feelings of wellness.

When new members are brought into our household I introduce them and briefly define each animal's or human animal's role or position. Animals often figure these things out a lot quicker than we humans; still, for me it is an issue of respect or common courtesy. All seemed to go well with the introductions and I was amazed at how quickly everyone accepted Kallee as a member of our family. It was around one o'clock in the morning that I realized that I had not defined positions or roles as clearly as I had thought.

"SQUWAAAAKK!!!!!" flutter, flutter, thud, bang, bang.

"What the. . ." said my half-awake husband.

"It's Popagolis!" I said as I hopped out of bed and raced down the hallway toward the living room, where his cage was kept. Popagolis was a parrot. "My God," I thought, "he was startled by something and has fallen." It took only seconds to reach his cage and in those few seconds I had already imagined the worst. My poor bird. I envisioned him lying on the bottom of his cage with a broken wing or worse yet, lifeless.

I flipped on the light with dread in my heart. Inside the cage, sitting on the bottom, was a green fluff of feathers. I was horrified and baffled at the sight. "Oh Popagolis!" I cried. Suddenly the green fluff shook and began to lay flat upon the body that held it together. A head formed, which carried with it a beak and two very wide, outraged eyes. The green fluff slowly took back the form of my little Amazon parrot.

"Are you okay?" I asked.

"She wants to eat me!" he squawked.

I followed his focus to find the perpetrator. On the floor to the side of his cage sat Kallee. Smugness covered her face. With a lift of her chin and flick of her tail she communicated, "I don't like what you serve and I'm hungry." My aristocratic avian friend could have fainted.

"Kallee, I understand that when you lived on the streets you had to hunt to survive. I also understand that hunting is instinctual for your species. You now have a home and with this home comes a few guidelines. The most important one is to live in respect and harmony with each other. I respect your instincts, but you will have to curb them when it comes to the members of this family. Are you willing to do this?"

Kallee looked at Popagolis and myself, expressing bafflement at the desire to have a bird as a family member. Then she said, "I will apologize to him." Popagolis smoothed his feathers the rest of the way and accepted the apology. But occasionally, if Kallee has her back to him and her tail is within reach, he

will reach for it, just to give her a little nip, to let her know he
has not forgotten.

PEACE AS YOU WALK YOUR WALK

He had a pictur-
esque life, blessed
by youth, health,
loving caregivers,
friends, and a sense
of purpose. He told me he was here to throw a spark into the
mundane. To keep things enlivened, fresh, and new. If things
got too serious, or a routine too stale, he would find some silly
antic to bring laughter into the picture. He was good at his job.
His caregivers thought of him as the barn jokester.

The five-year-old chestnut gelding was loving life. In the
morning he would be turned out to his gently rolling pastures

to enjoy the delicious grass and the company of a good horse companion. He loved being outside; there was so much for the senses to indulge in. He especially liked watching the activities of the farm. People were pulling up in their vehicles, some walking through the barn and visiting the horses inside. It was fun to check the people out. Occasionally a horse would leave or come back home. Then there were those silly dogs that lived on the property. They provided lots of entertainment. One of the dogs was constantly getting the others stirred up and interested in chasing something that didn't even exist. When the other dogs ran off, the small female dog that had started the chase stayed back and laughed. Zoom admired that dog. She knew how to have fun. In the evening Zoom was returned to the security and comfort of his stall, where he enjoyed grain and fresh hay.

One cold winter's morning, Zoom was let out into his pasture. Something happened that day that would change his perspective forever. No longer would he enjoy watching the dogs at play or see the sunlight sparkling on the dewy grass. Zoom's sunlight was gone.

Normally, Zoom would wait by the gate when it was getting close to time to return to the barn. This particular evening, Becky, the barn manager, was concerned when he wasn't waiting for her. She found him standing in the pasture with a stunned look on his face. Somehow she managed to get the disoriented and terrified horse back into his stall before calling the veterinarian.

The veterinarian confirmed Becky's worst fear. Zoom was completely blind. Tests were run and no cause was found for the blindness. To make matters worse, Zoom's terror was compounding. He would bump into the wall of his stall and react wildly; noises startled him just as badly. His fear was understandable but his reactions were very dangerous for his caregivers and himself. Because no cause could be found for the blindness, the doctors did not know what could be done for Zoom. Euthanasia was suggested as the best thing for him.

Becky and the owner of the farm wanted Zoom's input. So Becky called me, explaining the situation. "We just feel like there is still a purpose for Zoom. It is only right to get his input on this. He needs to know that we will support him through his process," Becky said.

"I agree," I replied. I quieted myself and tuned into Zoom. Feelings of utter devastation engulfed me. My heart went out to him.

"Zoom, I know this must be hard," I started.

"WHY?" came a pain-filled plea.

"I don't know. I do know that the answer will come to you if you ask it of the Universe."

A sense of bitterness washed over me. I allowed him to share those feelings. He knew the truth of my words and he was not ready to accept them at this time.

"You have good people who want to help you get through this. They cannot help you unless you calm down and allow them. You realize the consequences that a being with a body of your size can cause. When you interact with humans, you must be careful. I know that you care for these people."

"Yes," he answered.

"You must make the effort to control your physical body so that it does not jeopardize the safety of your people. If you cannot do this, or don't do this, they will send you to the spirit world. This is not what they want. Their desire is for you to remain and find your purpose."

"I understand," he communicated. He further communicated that he thought death would be a welcome release. "I am not sure I wish to remain under the current conditions of my body," he shared. I acknowledged his feelings and wished him peace.

"Becky," I said, "give him a little time to make his mind up. You'll know by his actions what his decision is. I think he may decide to come around and make peace with his challenge."

"I hope so. He's such a great horse," came Becky's reply.

"Let me know, or call if you just have questions," I added.

"Thanks, Patty. At least he knows we support him."

A week or so passed since I had talked with Zoom and his people. I was outside taking a walk with my dogs when Zoom came to mind. I wondered how he was doing, whether or not he'd decided to stay. In answer to my questions I felt Zoom's presence. He began communicating: "I am doing well, I have something to share with you, something that I want you to share with others as well." My surprise gave way to excitement and anticipation. I knew that whatever he was going to share was something I needed to write down, so I ran to my house to get pad and pen.

"As I walk now, there is mindfulness. I must slow down and experience life. All the smells, textures, and sounds. I'm coming to the knowledge that this is a gift I've been given. By being forced to slow down, I find what's really important. I must walk mindfully or I will bump into things or stumble. Only when I'm at peace and centered can I walk my walk.

"As I learn to accept my lesson, my hope is that others can use me as an example. Be mindful as you walk through life. Stay centered and aware, for if you allow fear or distress to influence you, you too will bump into obstacles rather than walk around them.

"I wish you peace as you walk your walk."

—Zoom, a horse, through Patty Summers

I called Becky to read her the message. To my delight she said Zoom had become much calmer. She had noticed a shift in him the day of my call. She invited me to visit Zoom the day he was going to be turned out into a special paddock just for him. It was a joyous day for us humans. Zoom was pretty happy too.

It wasn't long before Becky got the sense that Zoom would like a companion while he was out in his paddock. She had the perfect horse, Tequila, who was dubbed the "grandfather horse" and "gentle guardian." When I asked Zoom about Tequila he said he would be delighted for the company.

"I wonder if he'd like me to put a bell around Tequila's neck; that way he'd know where Tequila is at," Becky pondered.

I turned to Zoom and communicated the question.

"Are you kidding?" came the answer. "I can smell him coming." Through our laughter we knew that Zoom had regained his sense of humor.

I Heard What You Said, Now What Do You Mean?

For all the things we have in common, I must also keep in mind the animal's viewpoint and perspective. We don't always put importance on the same things. For example we humans put a great deal of emphasis on verbal language. I saw a "Far Side" cartoon once that said, "What you say to your dog." Under this caption was a picture of a man fussing at his dog, something like, "Lucky, you are a bad dog, look at the mess you caused...." On the other side the caption read: "What your dog hears." Under that caption was the man and dog, with the man saying, "Lucky, blah, blah, blah, blah. . . ." There is a lot of truth to that.

Animals do not put the same emphasis on the verbal. The communication they use is largely beyond verbal communication. As far as I am concerned, I am honored when an animal will communicate with words. When I get the communication in word form, I know that this is for my benefit, not theirs.

Quite often I am asked, "What does my animal think of me?" Or I'll hear someone say, "My dog thinks she's a person and I'm her mother." Generally speaking, animals know that we are human and that they are dogs, or whatever species they may be. I have noticed that the domestic animals take on some human characteristics or the characteristics of the species they are raised among. Similar to we human animals picking up the habits or traits of those with whom we associate or live.

At times an animal will refer to his or her person as Mom or Dad. My experience has been that "Mom" or "Dad" is more a term of endearment, kind of like saying Honey or Sweetheart. Some animals tell me they think of their people as Mom or Dad because the people refer to themselves that way. Then there are animals like Roxy.

Roxy is a pit bull/terrier mix who inherited the body of the pit bull and the wire-hair of the terrier. I think of Roxy having that carefree look. Her tousled gray with white coat reminds me of a person who has just woken up and hasn't combed her hair yet. She has no tail, so she makes up for it by wiggling her rear end. Roxy's person, Lynn, is a friend of mine, so I often have the pleasure of being greeted by Roxy's smiling eyes and wagging rear. Lynn calls Roxy her little powerhouse.

Lynn and I were talking about what animals call their people. "You know, I'd like to know what these guys call me," she said. At the time Lynn lived with two dogs, Roxy and her companion/brother Jasper, an Australian sheepdog mix. Roxy looked up, so I asked her first.

"Call her? I have no need to call her anything. She is my person, the one who loves and cares for me," came the perplexed reply. Before I could explain that all I was asking was if there was a term she used to refer to her person, Roxy had already turned to Jasper. "What do you call her?" she communicated to him. "Mom, stupid," Jasper commented.

Roxy was a sensitive dog, and I could feel that her feelings had been hurt, so I added, "Roxy, it is okay for you not to have a term to use for your person. I realize that your communication goes beyond verbal. We were just asking because some animals use verbal definitions at times. We were wondering if you did as well." My comment softened Jasper's. She shot him a look as he trotted off to go outside. Roxy sat down in contemplation.

Christmastime came and I was searching for a gift for Lynn. Knowing her love for the dogs, I decided a neat gift would be an offer of my services as translator for the dogs. I would get a message to Lynn from Jasper and Roxy and put it into writing. I went to each one and asked if they would like to share something with Lynn. "Would you like to tell her what you think of your home, or share anything about your life with her?" Roxy was quick to answer "YES!" She was very excited.

"Mom," she started, "I have decided to call you Mom. Is that okay? It's not that I didn't love you before, I just wasn't sure what to call you. . . . I know I act silly sometimes, but life is supposed to be fun, Mom. I like to make you happy. I think Jasper is too serious, but I love my big brother. If I could give you something, it would be a big smile on your face." Roxy's face was filled with pride and satisfaction. She imaged to me herself standing before her beloved "Mom," face beaming with love, and wiggling her rear.

Adapting to human communication is something I found Tasha, a German shepherd, particularly skilled at. Her person called me to communicate with both of his German shepherds. Tasha was the older shepherd and Maggie the younger. Tom commented on Tasha's wonderful manners.

"She is a true lady," he told me. Maggie, although lovely, had some growing up to do.

"She is full of herself," I told Tom.

Tom was a bit frustrated with Maggie's reactions toward the cats that shared her home. She loved to pick on them.

Before I got the chance to discuss this matter with Maggie, Tom interjected, "Ask Tasha what she thinks about Maggie's interactions with the cats." I was taken aback by Tasha's comment, "She is disrespectful of her toys." I decided I somehow was not clear, so I imaged the cats again to her. With a bit of irritation she communicated again, "She is disrespectful of her toys." Does she think I am talking about stuffed animals? I asked myself. I thought I had been clear in imaging the cats walking around. Then it hit me to ask Tasha what a "toy" was. "A toy is something he gives us for our enjoyment; we are to take care of our toys," she answered.

I asked Tom what he told them about toys. Almost verbatim he said, "They are here for the dogs to enjoy, but they must take care of them."

"And the cats?" I asked.

"Well," he replied, "actually I told them pretty much the same thing."

I shared with Tom what Tasha had said. It made sense when I thought about it. Tasha knew the cats were living beings. It reminded me of speaking a foreign language when we may get the words crossed with the definition. I appreciated her attempt to accommodate me by sharing in my language.

As for Maggie, Tom and I talked about her need to be recognized for her uniqueness. Tasha was like the straight-A student and Maggie was the athlete. Her teasing the cats was simply a way to gain attention. She felt Tom did not care for her as much as he did Tasha. "He loves you for different reasons. His love for you is no less, just unique, as you are unique," I told her. She listened, pondered, and then acknowledged that this made sense. She said she enjoyed being unique.

Perhaps the best known for adapting to and utilizing human communication would be our fine feathered friends, the birds. It is well known that parrots have some ability to communicate to us physically in our language. When I was asked to give a talk to a bird club, I met an interesting yellow napped Amazon. These birds are known for their verbal abilities. Tara was mostly green, with yellow feathers sprinkled on her head. Her person, Susan, worked for an aviary that had asked me to come and communicate with the birds there. Susan wanted me to find out why Tara continued to chase and try to attack Susan's husband.

Tara had come to live with her when Susan was a child still at home with her parents. When her parents divorced, the bird remained with Susan's father and Susan lived with her mother. According to Susan, her father was unkind to Tara, picking at her and teaching her bad language. Once Susan moved out and got married, she took Tara to live with her. Susan and her husband Brian knew Tara did not like men, thanks to Susan's father, and yet they had hoped that in time she would adjust to Brian.

"All's fine until Brian gets home. Then she jumps off her cage onto the floor and chases Brian, saying, 'Do you want an ass whipping?'"

"You're kidding," I said, trying to keep from laughing out loud.

"No," Susan said.

Through the communication Tara related to me that she liked Brian. The chasing had become a game.

"They (Susan and Brian) think it's funny," related the bird.

Susan had a guilty look on her face; then she broke out in laughter. "She's right, we do think it's funny. We think she's funny in general and smart, let me tell you. I had her in a carrier outside one day. She didn't have a perch inside this carrier so she had nothing for her feet to grip on to. A strong gust of wind came along and knocked Tara off balance. Tara got up, shook herself and said to the wind, 'Do you want an ass whipping?'" Laughter broke out in the room.

"Tell her about the time you brought Tara over for a visit and it was just us girls," said Susan's boss, the owner of the aviary.

"Oh yeah," began Susan. "There were about four of us, all women, sitting in this room talking. It got quiet and all of the sudden Tara says in a very soft voice, as if confessing, 'Ass whip's a bad word.'"

By now I was laughing so hard tears were rolling down my cheeks. I looked over toward the bird. Tara cocked her head a bit so she could bring me into full focus and said physically to me, "Do YOU want an ass whipping?"

"No ma'am," I answered quickly.

POPAGOLIS SPEAKS

Big things come in little pack-
ages. Boy, does that fit for my little
parrot friend. Popagolis—Pop for
short—is a red lored Amazon, one of
the smaller breeds in the Amazon
family. Mostly green feathers cover his body, although his face
is decorated with bright yellow feathers on the sides of his beak
and brilliant red travels from the top of his beak between his
eyes. His head is lightly sprinkled with lavender feathers.
Looking into his eyes, you can see the fire of his personality.

Pop had always been a little feisty since he first came to live
with us ten years ago. He came as a baby and, after I found out

his background, I figured he'd had to develop such a fiery personality in order to survive. I asked him once what he thought of Ereenie, our sweet tabby cat. "She's a wimp," he communicated. Ereenie, overhearing, said, "He's pompous." Most would agree with Ereenie's description.

It was not until Pop came to live with us that I realized the importance of learning how a bird was first acquired. Tropical birds like Amazons are either wild caught or captive raised, the preferred method being captive raised. Many wild-caught birds are killed in the process; others suffer other repercussions from the cruelty they are subject to. Pop had been wild caught and the guilt I carried when I found this out was, needless to say, immense.

When I asked Pop about his background, he said he did not have a strong memory of his parent birds. He remembered being high in a tree. Then his parents disappeared when the men came. "It happened so fast," he said. "All I knew was I needed and wanted to be fed." I was horrified as he sent me an image of himself as a baby bird, frightened and hungry. For a long time my guilt haunted me. Ignorance had been this bird's enemy. I was ignorant before he came into my life and now his ignorance of the wild prevented him from being released back into his native home.

Pop was never one to make you feel sorry for him. At a young age he exuded quite the air of confidence. Often he would nip and fuss, always wanting things on his terms. What a pistol he could be. For the most part I did not mind. He was entitled, I thought. It wasn't until Pop grew older and his nips turned into full-blown bites that I minded. I think the final straw came the day he decided to get ahead of the upcoming fashion trend of body piercing. Apparently he thought I needed a ring near my lip: body piercing, parrot style. I can laugh about it now; at the time it was quite painful, both physically and emotionally.

In time my physical pain became a distant memory. My emotional pain still remained. "He doesn't love me," I thought. "He hates me because of his capture. I should have been more educated about how birds are acquired. I was so unthinking." I was engulfed with a feeling of guilt and remorse. "I deserve this. How could I expect him to love me?" I began shutting down when I was near him. Joe watched as my relationship with the bird began to deteriorate.

"Patty, you have got to do something. This is not fair to you or Pop. Either find him another home or work something out," he said. I knew he was right.

"Well, it's obvious to me he wants another home," I said. I knew inside that I had come to this conclusion not through communicating with Popagolis, but because of my own emotional state. My feelings of guilt were speaking. Far away I heard another answer, an answer I was not ready to hear yet. I decided to call a fellow animal communicator for her assistance.

"Patty," she said, "this bird does not want another home. He cannot fathom that. He loves you and he feels a part of you. He says his biting is his way of showing affection for you."

I closed my eyes and breathed in a deep sigh of relief. "Well," I said, "I'm glad to hear this. The fact is I did not want to find him another home and yet I was not going to make him stay with me if he was unhappy. The only thing is, he will have to find other ways to show me affection."

The animal communicator laughed. "I agree. He says he will try instead to make a kissing sound to you, but he wants you to know that it is his instinct to bite and it will be hard to fight against instinct."

"At least this is a start," I said.

I believe animals choose their people to help teach them or to enhance their person's life experience. Pop came to teach me many things. The first was a very important lesson concerning animal communication: Do not allow your personal feelings or emotions to interfere with the communication. Judgments or personal feelings will cloud the communication, not allowing the animal's perspective to come through.

Through the understanding and acceptance of this lesson, I was then able to communicate again with Pop, with emphasis on rebuilding our relationship. The understanding of Popagolis's perspective gave me more patience and acceptance.

He did try to curb his instinctual behavior. There were times, however, when his efforts were greater than others, and I seemed to be picking up something else from him.

When someone tells me they will "try" to do something, there is space left for failure. What was his reason for choosing to "try"? From what I knew of birds, some biting behavior was instinctual. I wondered if he was forgetting that my skin was not protected by a coat of feathers and therefore could not take the force of his bites. A part of me knew that there was something else that needed to be addressed: my guilt.

I looked at Popagolis with tear-filled eyes. "I am so sorry," I said. It was not as if he hadn't heard me say this before. From the time I learned about his background, our relationship was filled with "I'm sorry's." They were all heartfelt, but this time I knew I must make peace with this guilt. If I could not, he and I would never be able to have a healthy relationship. Pop looked at me, cocked his head and said both verbally and telepathically, "I love you." Now the tears began to gush down my face. "You did nothing knowingly to harm me. I am supposed to be here with you. We are a part of each other," he added. He saw nothing to forgive; the forgiveness needed was for myself. Forgiveness has been a difficult gift to offer myself. This bird made the importance of giving myself that gift very clear, yet another lesson he came to teach me.

Popagolis shares a message for bird lovers.

"For those who find a kinship with the winged ones: You are drawn to us for a reason. Take a closer look at us. We capture the colors of the rainbows in our feathers. Our brilliant colors are symbolic of the brightness of our being. We fly close to the sun, knowing its warmth and life-giving energy, and we know the exhilaration of flight. The wind is our brother, carrying us to new heights. Our keen vision brings things into focus quickly. Our feathers are soft, but our hearts courageous. Many of us are willing to share these qualities with you. Remember who we are, your winged brothers and sisters. And for those of you who have brought us into your homes, your companions. Do not forget what has drawn you to us in the first place. You have shared with others your love for my kind, now teach others of our qualities, so that they may understand why you love."

—Popagolis, a bird, through Patty Summers

PROUD TO BE YOUR DOG

Leadership is a role that is played throughout the animal kingdom, including human animals. I remember going to a beautiful farm in Virginia. Amongst others in its animal family, there lived seven English setters. The people were concerned about their young female setter named Clairol. Her longish hair had a base of white with black spots over much of her body, referred to as "ticking." Her face was a striking brown, highlighted with what looked like black eyeliner. Her people's concern was about Clairol's field trial training. At first she had been doing well. "She showed great enthusiasm and promise," said Lindy, Clairol's female person. "Then all of the sudden she started acting shy and submissive, as if she had done something wrong."

Sitting in the den of this lovely country homestead, it was obvious that the animals in this home were very much a part of the family. Upon the bookshelf were framed photos of horses and dogs, along with various books on canine and equine care. A wicker basket on the floor held all the dog toys a canine could want. Joining us humans were several of the seven setters, some sitting on furniture, some on the floor chewing on toys or bones.

I turned to Clairol and tuned in to find out what was wrong. I could sense conflict and frustration, as she communicated, "I can't do it."

"Why not?" I asked. "Your people said you were doing so well."

"She won't let me," the answer came. I followed the direction of Clairol's stare and was abruptly halted at what I encountered. A large female setter displayed herself on a chair with the dignity of a queen. She raised her black and white head, looked at me and said, "I am the head female dog here. No one does better than me." All the dog needed to make this scene complete was a gavel in her paw to hit upon her bench as she passed down her law.

I blinked, trying to regain my composure, and began to share what had just transpired with the dog's humans. In the middle of telling Lindy and Bill about the queen's communication, I felt a cold stare, accompanied by hostility. Lindy and Bill noticed as well.

"She's angry at you for sharing her secrets, isn't she?" Lindy said with amusement. "Did she just curse you?"

"Essentially yes," I answered. I wasn't surprised to find out that this grand dame's name was Queenie. "How appropriate," I commented.

I tuned into Queenie and began. "I honor your position in this pack. If you feel I was disrespectful I apologize; however, there needs to be some resolution to this situation and your people had a right to know what was going on." I felt some of her hostility toward me soften as she felt my sincerity in honoring and acknowledging her position. After a moment she agreed to continue communicating with me.

She shared that she adored her male person, Bill, and would do anything for him. She loved Lindy as well, but Bill was her favorite. Bill and she were almost inseparable, her loyalty a credit to her species. She lived to please him and to be the best dog she could for him. She saw in Clairol the personality of a leader—competition, reason for concern. She had to squelch any competition. With Queenie's permission I shared this information with her humans.

Bill said, "Patty, you tell Queenie that there is no way another dog could take her place. She will always be tops in my eyes."

"I recognize her status as well," added Lindy.

I relayed to Queenie the feelings of her people. Pride filled the dog's being. I then proceeded, communicating, "A good leader respects those with her. A good leader knows that it takes everyone's gifts or talents to make the whole. Bill and Lindy see you as the head female. You say you would do anything for Bill. Well it would make him and Lindy happy for Clairol to reach her potential. It would also make your pack stronger."

Queenie digested this a moment and then said to Clairol, "Do your best." Clairol accepted Queenie's blessing with grace.

I encouraged Clairol to "be all she could be." Queenie commanded respect, not out of fear, but out of an essence about her. She had an air about her, as would a world leader or one of royal blood.

Later Bill and Lindy reported that Clairol was doing great in the fieldwork. As for Queenie, she was back to enjoying her rightful name.

From working in more mainstream animal care, I found a common theme of dominance when training dogs. There are aspects behind this sort of training that relate somewhat to animal communication. The idea behind the human acting like the alpha or top dog is so the dog understands from his or her perspective who is in charge. It is good that we humans are making an effort to relate to animals more on their terms, although sometimes I feel that the point is missed. That is why a dog comes into our lives in the first place: to be our companion or working partner. Often people look at animals as servants to humankind. I do not believe that animals are servants. Rather, if they have chosen to work with humans, they come in service. To be truly in service is an ultimate spiritual and honorable space. Animals are masters at this. The animal and plant kingdoms give so much and ask so little. This giving is done freely, without conditions. We are the ones who lose when we do not recognize and acknowledge their gifts.

I had the privilege of knowing a German shepherd named Molly. The fur on her body was mostly brown, with black lightly brushing her back, and her black muzzle enhancing her brown face. Intense eyes expressed the seriousness for which Molly took her job of companion and watchdog to her person.

Molly passed into the spirit world at a young age due to health reasons. In her short life she gave her all to her person, who she referred to as Mom. She expressed to me the joy that watching over her home brought to her. Nothing went on outdoors or indoors that Molly was unaware of. Her keen ears and eyes were always alert. Molly could put on a show of vicious protection of her home and, although she balanced that with great friendliness, I felt that, should she sense real danger, she would do what she must to protect her person. Molly carried the heart of her German shepherd heritage. Service and loyalty to her Mom was a task she rallied to, as she related in a communication she shared before her passing. As she communicated this to me she sent an image of a shepherd in all her glory, sitting tall, chest out and head held high.

> *"As a puppy I looked at you and felt your warmth and love. This would be my person, I told myself. I knew that you would care for me and I would have no worries about my care. I felt safe and loved as a pup, I knew you would do anything for me. I am older now and have responsibilities. I will watch over our home and make sure you don't have a single worry about things going unguarded. Mom, I want you to know I am proud to be your dog."*
>
> —Molly, a dog, through Patty Summers

As I sit writing this I look down at my feet to see my companion Mauvree. I look into her soft brown eyes, feeling the love my black Labrador friend sends to me. I asked Mauvree once what was her favorite thing to do. "Anything I can do with you," she answered.

"Who am I to deserve such love, such loyalty?" I ask.

"My person," she answers. I close my eyes in reverent gratitude.

WE CHOOSE
OUR PATH

I found the cool autumn breeze refreshing as I stepped out of my car into the parking lot at the animal shelter. I was returning from lunch, wishing I could spend the rest of the day in the mountains hiking. "Oh well," I thought to myself, "maybe I'll get a chance this weekend." I sighed and headed inside the building.

Inside, activity flowed as usual. The lobby hosted a woman and her young son. Both mother and son were peering over the counter into the office at a chubby black puppy waddling on the floor. The attractive woman with dark blonde hair was filling out an adoption contract as her son of about eight years was giggling with delight and saying, "I can't wait to get him home." I smiled at them as I walked past.

I hoped that the boy would always feel that way about his new friend. It was difficult not to be a little cynical after working in an animal shelter. Too often we would witness great enthusiasm from a family when adopting an animal, especially a puppy or a kitten. Not many can resist the charms of baby animals. When those animals grew older, losing that look of innocence and charm they once possessed, they would become less appealing to their humans. No longer were they "adorable." Now they were too much responsibility or, worse, a nuisance.

It was not unusual to have people bring an adult dog into the humane society, saying that the animal had grown too large or that it no longer fit into their lifestyles. Then, once they finished filling out the required paperwork to leave the animal with us, they would turn around and ask to see our puppies with the intention of adopting one. Because our shelter felt it was important to place our animals in homes that were permanent, it was the shelter's policy not to adopt to people who surrendered their own animals to us, unless the circumstances were extreme.

I continued out of the lobby into the hallway and entered the office that I shared with the manager of the shelter. He had stepped out so I was alone. "Think positive, Patty," I told myself. "Put it out there that this pup will grow into a loving and lifetime relationship with this family." Putting my things down on my desk, I smiled as I looked at the pictures there. They were photos of animals who, despite their unlikeliness to find homes, did so. Against what seemed impossible odds, these animals had found wonderful, loving homes. I kept the photos to remind me of why I was working there.

In one photo was Buffy, an elderly cat who enjoyed the luxury of the indoors until her elderly people passed on and the adult children moved in, kicking Buffy outdoors. A neighbor felt sorry for the cat, who stood outside wailing pitifully to go back indoors, and brought the now homeless cat into the shelter.

As the months went by I began to wonder if Buff would ever find a home. A feisty, cranky old gal who didn't much care for people, Buff was less than appealing to most people. Although our shelter did euthanize, there were no time limits put on the animals who came to live there. Animals were kept as long as there was room, and as long as their health and personality were not a threat to themselves or others. Finally a woman in her early thirties happened to come in with a friend who had come to adopt another cat. She laid eyes on Buff, heard her story and fell in love. The photo on my desk, sent by her new person, showed the cat comfortably displayed on her new couch.

Then there were Keech and Isis, mother and daughter dogs, whose people said simply when bringing the dogs in, "They are too much trouble and by the way we think Isis is pregnant." Upon their arrival at the shelter the collie/chow mixes shot us bizarre looks, as if we were some sort of space aliens. I asked them what was wrong. "You look strange," Keech told me. It took a moment before I realized Keech was referring to my skin color. Darker-skinned humans had raised her and Isis. Apparently they had never had contact with light-skinned people. I smiled, saying, "Yes. Just like your species, my species comes in different colors, too."

The dogs took guarding their territory seriously, barking at every stranger. Once they were introduced they usually settled down; however, it was virtually impossible to introduce them to everyone. Therefore the dogs gave the wrong impression that they were vicious. To make matters worse, the dogs wished to be adopted together. Finding someone who was willing to adopt two dogs at once was a rarity.

Isis was indeed pregnant. She gave birth to three fuzzy pups about three weeks after coming to live at the shelter. By some miracle the pups survived, despite being raised in an animal shelter, not the healthiest of environments. We were careful to ensure clean living quarters, yet due to the number of inhabitants sometimes, accidental contact would be made; airborne disease was also a constant threat. Many of the animals were strays coming from God knows what kind of background, some being diseased and some carriers of disease. Still, these three fuzzy little guys not only survived, but also received homes once they were old enough to leave their mother.

A week or so after the pups got adopted, a middle-aged couple came in looking for two dogs for companions. We liked the people and introduced them to the mother and daughter. The husband in the couple was attracted to Keech, the wife Isis. To my delight the dogs warmed up quickly to these people. Later I received the photo of two happy dogs playing in their new backyard with their family. "Yeah," I nodded to the photos, "think positive."

I needed to get back to work and check to see if any new animals had come in since lunch. I left the office to go into the main area where the chubby pup had just been. As I entered, the family was walking out the front door. The boy was cuddling his pup, talking to him. "Come on, you cute little guy. I'm going to take great care of you," he said.

"Nice kid," Page said to me.

"Good," I smiled at her. "Anybody new come in?"

"Yessss," Page answered with a grimace on her face. "These people brought in a lovely German shepherd who has suffered abuse. They have had the dog for a few weeks. He used to belong to their neighbor, who was the abuser. They took the dog in to get him away from the neighbor, but the fact is, they can't handle him. He is rather aggressive."

As she spoke she picked up the paperwork the people had filled out upon surrendering him to the shelter. She handed me the paper on which the dog's history was written. There was nothing new on the paperwork that she hadn't already shared with me. "I had them put him in an outside run," Page added as I was glancing over the form.

"Well, I'll go out and visit him," I said.

"Be careful," she called as I left the room.

Fallen leaves that danced with the wind on the sidewalk greeted me as I stepped outdoors. I turned to face the chain-linked dog runs, which were connected to the metal building. He was the only dog out there. The rest of the dogs were inside. I was captivated by how handsome he was. His body size was small for a shepherd, yet his features were in proportion. He wore a shiny black coat trimmed in brown on his feet and touches of brown on his face. In his eyes I could see the brutality that had befallen him. But there was still a longing to reach out to someone. He was caught between expressing the love and loyalty that only a dog could for his people and the fear of loving only to be devastated once again. My heart went out to him.

I sat down on the sidewalk outside of his run. A low growl came from the dog's throat as he watched me with distrustful eyes. I looked away from him, not wanting him to take my actions as a challenge. I quieted myself and began to communicate to him. "I'm Patty. I work in this place. It is a place that animals come to when they do not have their own personal people to care for them. My job and the job of the others working here is to assist animals in finding new people."

The dog continued to growl as he sent an image of a man standing over him. The man was angry and yelling as he whipped the dog with what looked like a leash of some kind. The dog crouched, eyes squinting, as the man continued to whip him numerous times. I flinched, my stomach turned. "No, no one will do that to you here," I said with conviction. The growling stopped, but the suspicious looks still came from his lowered head. "Well buddy, you can't stay out here. We need to go back to Isolation and get you something to eat," I said out loud, as I imaged my intentions to him. The growling started again and I heard, "I am not going anywhere with you."

I did not expect him to trust me immediately. Trust would take time. Unfortunately I could not leave him outside while he learned to trust the other staff members or me. The public had access to the outside runs and the shepherd made it quite clear that biting someone was not beyond him. Slowly I stood up and went to get a restraining pole. I normally did not care to use a restraining pole, but with an animal who was frightened or aggressive, it provided the handler with safety and gave the animal a comfort zone from the person. If used properly it was essentially a stiff leash. I opened the dog's run door and communicated what the pole was for and what I was doing with it. He growled, but to my relief he stood still while I gently slipped the noose part of the pole over his neck. He followed me out of his run and down the sidewalk to Isolation, still keeping me in his watchful eye.

We made it to a small concrete dog run, where a stainless steel bucket and bowl waited for him with food and water. I removed the restraining pole standing outside his run. "I would like to be a friend," I communicated. "Think about it. I'll be back." As I left Isolation I turned to look at the shepherd once more to reassure him that he was safe. I sensed confusion, not fear.

I went to the food storage room in search of dog treats. I found a box of biscuits and headed back to Isolation, where I found the dog sniffing his food. He stopped to keep me in his eyesight. "Peace offering," I said as I shoved a biscuit through the chain-link gate and dropped it into his run. He eyeballed the treat but did not pick it up. I decided he'd had enough for the day, so I left, hoping he would take me up on my offer of friendship.

It took several days of communicating with him and bribing him with treats before he trusted me enough to allow me to put a leash on him so that he could go on a walk. During our first walk together, the protective walls guarding his wounded heart came crashing down. He decided he could love me; I could be his friend. His need to be totally devoted to someone was sad and touching at the same time—sad, because his devotion sometimes blurred his reason. He often found other people to be threats to his person and would defend his person, or think he was, with a vengeance. I could not have the dog outside of his run, unless he was on leash or away from strangers. If he saw a stranger he would more often than not charge. I communicated to him that his suspicions were often unfounded. He made considerable progress, although the fact that the shelter was a place open to the public made caution a necessity.

Interest in the dog was not a problem. When he was inevitably spotted as I was walking him inside on my way back to Isolation, people would comment or ask about him. A handsome purebred dog was a coveted adoption. The problem was finding the right kind of home for him. The shelter manager had already disapproved of me seeking a home for the dog, due to his aggressive tendencies. He suggested putting the dog to sleep. I understood the policy but I also was known for stretching policy a bit, most of the time with success. If I felt the animal wanted that chance, I would do what I could to provide it. I told Sirius, as I now called him, of his options. He would have to work on his suspicious nature, or I would be unable to find him a new home. He would be sent to the spirit world.

I strongly considered adopting the shepherd myself. Before bringing a new animal home, I always check with the ones at home to clear it with them. Then I let the new animal know about my family. All was fine until I told Sirius about my cats. To my horror, I received an image of the dog chasing and killing my oldest male cat. His instinct and desire to kill cats was great, too great for me to risk my cat family. He remained in Isolation while we kept our eyes and ears open for the right kind of person, preferably someone who understood the breed and lived in the country. It did not take long.

"Patty," Mandy said, "there's a man here who's looking for a companion for his German shepherd. He seems very nice and he lives in the country," she smiled, anticipating. "No cats."

"Where is he?" I asked.

She pointed out a tall young man in his late twenties with short hair and glasses. I walked up to him.

"I understand you are looking for a dog," I said.

"Yes," he replied, "I have a female German shepherd. She goes with me on hikes, but I feel like she'd like a companion, especially while I'm at work."

"What would her companion do while you and she went on hikes?" I asked, not wanting the dog to be left out.

"Oh, whoever I adopt will be just as much part of the family as Sarah is," he answered.

There was a softness about the man. I told him about my buddy in the back. He wanted to meet him and I cautioned about the dog's possible aggression. The shepherd looked at the man cautiously, but no growl came from him. I communicated to the dog that this was a potential person for him and that he had a female shepherd as well. My friend liked the idea of having a dog companion. Like myself, the man was drawn to the dog.

"I really like him," he said. "Something about him is so appealing. Can I bring my dog by tomorrow so that they can meet?"

"Sure, I think that would be best. It will also give you two more time to get acquainted," I answered.

The next day the man showed up with his dog. Sarah was much bigger than Sirius. She was the more traditionally marked tan and black. The dogs hit it off immediately. We decided to turn them loose in the side yard so they could play more freely. The man smiled as he watched the two chase each other around.

"I want to adopt him. What's the procedure?" he asked.

"You understand that due to his background his reaction to people sometimes is unpredictable? You don't have to treat him with kid gloves, yet you do need to keep this in mind."

"I totally understand that," he replied.

I tuned into Sirius, "Is this okay with you?" Even though I knew the answer, I still needed to ask. "Yes," came the reply.

Tears filled my eyes the day Sirius's new person came to pick him up. At first Sirius hesitated, looking at me. Then he saw Sarah, and out he bounded toward her. A bittersweet feeling entered my heart as I watched my friend hop into his new family's vehicle. The man stopped and said to me, "I know you love him. I will bring him back for a visit sometime."

"You do that," I smiled.

A couple of weeks went by and the man was true to his word. We went out to the side yard again, so Sirius would not have to go into the building. The happy dog bounded along with the man on one side and Sarah on the other. He began telling me how much he loved Sirius in addition to how well he was fitting in. I only half-listened, as I was busy watching my friend. A pang of jealousy hit me at the loss of that special relationship that I had shared with the dog. The dog doesn't love me anymore, I thought, and that hurts a bit. In the midst of my self-pity the dog picked up my thoughts. He ran toward me, stopping for a moment to lick my face. "I still love you," he said, "and I'll never forget you. It's just that I have a new person now. Thank you for bringing us together." He was right. Our relationship had served its purpose. This was something to rejoice about. After Sirius's visit I no longer missed him; rather, I thought of him with fondness.

A month went by. Then I was told that Sirius and the man were in the front lobby and wished to see me. Entering the room excitedly, I was met with immediate feelings of anguish. The man's face reflected deep emotional pain. Had Sirius not been standing beside him I would have thought he had come to tell me the dog was dead. According to the man, Sirius had snapped at his landlord. Apparently, while Sirius's people were out, the landlord had entered the house to repair something. The man said that he was not aware the landlord was coming or he would have done something with Sirius to avoid any potential problem.

"But, with you not at home, Sirius was just doing what was natural, protecting his property," I said defensively.

"I know that," said the man. "I told that to the landlord, but he says he doesn't care. Sirius goes or we have to move."

I wanted to say, "THEN MOVE!" I knew it was not my place to tell this man how to live his life, so I kept my mouth shut. As if the man read my thoughts, he said, "Moving at this time for my wife and I is out of the question." I did not say a word, but simply picked up a surrender form and asked him to fill it out.

The man had tears in his eyes as he left Sirius. "Do you think you can find him another home?" he asked.

"I don't know. The fact that he snapped at your landlord is not encouraging. I'll do what I can."

"I am sorry, Sirius," he said as he patted the dog on the head. Sirius whined as the man walked out the door. He pulled hard on the lead, trying to go with him. I felt the sorrow in the dog's heart. I led him back to an open dog run. At first he stood at the gate whining and looking toward the entranceway. He was looking for his person. "He's not coming back, Sirius," I communicated.

I explained as best I could why the man was not coming back, but how do you explain to a dog that he can no longer live with a person because he was doing his job? I mostly just told him that it wasn't his fault, that he was still loved by the man and me. After a while Sirius came and sat beside me, licking my face.

"I wish I had adopted you myself," I said. Then another image of my cat, dead, shown in my mind's eye. I thought about ways I could keep Sirius secure so that the cats would be safe. No, that was not the answer. The cat I kept seeing killed was not afraid of dogs. Even if the dog was secured, the cat would most likely cross his path sooner or later. Freeman, a name that fit the cat well, was not known for prudence. In addition to this, it would not be a quality life for Sirius, not a life he wanted.

Several days went by before a man with dark hair and a stocky build saw Sirius and inquired about him. "There is just something about the dog that is quite appealing," he went on.

"I know," I said.

I personally did not like this man as well as the first one who'd adopted Sirius. He was a bit cocky, with a tough exterior. But Sirius thought this man was "fun."

"Well," I told the dog, "he wouldn't be my choice, yet I am not a young male dog. I can see why you would like him. As long as you are happy and he is good to you, well, that is what is important." The dog wagged his tail.

After questioning the man further, I felt he would be good to the dog. In some ways he made a better match for the dog than the first person. Even though he had a tough side, I could see the softness in his heart. I formally filled out Sirius's adoption papers. We had our goodbyes, with this man promising to bring the dog back for a visit. The dog trotted off with the man.

I was uncertain—not about the man, but about Sirius. Would the dog be able to respond rather than react? I knew he understood the difference, but sometimes it was as if he did not care. His background had warped his sense of balance. Had I expected too much from the dog? Would he choose to overcome his past? A month passed before I got my answer.

"He's a heartbreaker," said the man in obvious grief. I stood numbly as he told me how Sirius had been doing so well, but had then started chasing livestock on the neighboring property. "That we were working on," explained the man. "Then out of nowhere he snapped at a child. If I hadn't been right there. . . ." His voice trailed off. "I do love him. I wish it hadn't come to this."

"Me too." My voice was barely audible.

"He was right," I said to myself. I was thinking of the manager's advice not to try to find someone to adopt this dog. "He is too much of a risk," he had said. "I'll give you a shot at it, but you know the policy."

Yes, I knew the policy. I had felt the dog wanted a chance and deserved it. I now faced the cold, hard reality.

I knew Sirius's fate. A part of me wanted to walk out of that animal shelter and never walk back in. I knew that did not change anything. Whether I was there or not, someone would carry out that fate. I took him outside for one last run in the side yard. "I will be releasing you to the spirit world, my friend. I no longer have a choice, and if this has to be done then let it be by my hands. I should have let you go when you first came in, I guess. I feel I have allowed more emotional torture to befall you. I only wanted to see you happy." Quiet resignation came from the dog. We finished playing together for the last time as Sirius and Patty. He followed me into a private room. "Please forgive me," I cried. I gave him the lethal injection and he left this plane of existence. I held his limp body in my arms and wept. Never in my life had I ever felt such feelings of betrayal, cruelty, and utter pain. I had killed my friend.

Depression became my companion for the next several months. Try as I might, I could make no sense of what had transpired. I had always believed that things happened for a reason. There seemed no reason for this. I could not forgive myself; there was no peace in my heart. I spent many a night sitting on my front porch staring at the night sky asking, "Why? What could I have done differently?" On one of these sleepless nights, I was sitting on the porch and questioning the Universe. Instead of the normal cold emptiness, I felt as if a soft, warm blanket surrounded me. A gentle presence approached. I turned to see Kallee, my tabby cat.

"Patty, we are not helpless beings," she communicated. She sensed my confusion and continued. "We (animals) choose our destiny as well." I realized suddenly that she was talking about Sirius and my feelings of guilt toward him.

"But I do have a responsibility to the animals," I said.

"Yes," she agreed, "a responsibility to respect us as living beings. As living beings we are not helpless. We also make choices. The dog chose his."

"You are telling me he chose to die?" I said with disbelief.

"Sometimes choices are on a subconscious level, and still all are choices. In this case Sirius had the option of staying in his adopted home. He instead decided to come back and help a beloved friend."

The cat now had me utterly confused. "What?"

"Since Sirius's passing into the spirit world, have you not made some life-changing decisions?" she asked. I paused to think. She was right. For some time I had considered leaving the shelter. The emotional price tag for working there had grown too high. Only my love for the animals and desire to help them kept me there. Sirius's death made me reluctant to continue paying that emotional price. I had come to the realization that I could best help the animals by doing my communication work. Humans needed to remember that they are connected to the animals. Through that connection the animals would gain the respect they deserve. "Your sense of loyalty would not let you leave the shelter easily," Kallee communicated. "It took something of this magnitude to get you to decide to leave."

A wave of guilt swept over me again. "Why would anyone agree to die so I'd move on?" I asked. "Am I that dense?"

"The shelter had served its purpose on your path. Part of the dog's path intertwined with yours. For you, going forth is not only what is best for you, it is the highest way for you to serve the animals." The volume of her communication hit me.

I had been unable to communicate with Sirius's spirit until that moment. I felt his joy beyond words. His handsome face filled my mind's eye. I opened my eyes and looked into the starry sky.

"I am honored." I said to the one I know as the brightest of the stars.

THE TRANSCENDING POWER OF LOVE

The paper read, "Man Hires Private Plane to Search for Missing Dog." Sheba, an elderly Labrador mix, and her person Don had become the topic of the town. For seventeen years the yellow dog enjoyed a quiet life; now she was famous. Don's love and loyalty to Sheba was apparent. He left no stone unturned in his search for her. People could not help but be moved as they heard his story and saw the desperation and pain in his eyes.

I too was touched by the man's earnest search, although communicating with the lost is not my favorite thing to do. Animals share with me only their point of view, which realistically is not always that helpful in locating them. Animals do not tell me they are on Maple Street. They may show me woods or perhaps a house. Sometimes the locations I am shown could be almost anywhere. Then there is the possibility that the animal has died. To tell someone that his or her dear friend has died is very hard on both the person and me.

Due to the media attention concerning Sheba, I must admit that my curiosity got the best of me and I did tune into her. Because she told me she had passed into spirit, I decided that if Don was supposed to hear this from me, somehow the Universe or Sheba would send him. Only a few days after I had communicated with Sheba, I received a phone call.

"Is this Patty Summers?" came the question from a soft masculine voice.

"Yes," I answered. He did not need to tell me who he was. The despair in his voice did.

"I understand you can talk to animals," he said. Plans were made for a consult with Sheba.

It was a warm summer evening and we decided to sit outside on a deck. I was grateful to be outdoors; nature always gives me a sense of strength. I needed that now, as I prepared to share something that was going to bring more sorrow to another.

"Patty, anything you can tell me about where she might be—" he began.

I nodded, about to share what Sheba had told me, when I noticed he was studying my face.

"You've already talked to her, haven't you?" he asked.

"Yes," I said, my voice barely audible.

"She's dead, isn't she?"

"Yes," I answered, but he did not wait for my answer. He had already begun sobbing, crying out her name. My heart went out to him. He lowered his head and covered it with his hands.

After a few minutes he asked, "Did she tell you where she went? I'd like to find her body and bury it."

"She said she went to the woods. It was one of her favorite places to go and she thought it was a peaceful place."

Don smiled. "Yeah, there are woods behind our house and she did love to go in them. Patty, I feel I caused her to leave. I was out working on a motorcycle and it backfired. Sheba was afraid of gunfire, so she took off when she heard the motorcycle. If only I had not been working on that damn motorcycle. . . ." His voice trailed off and he began to cry again.

I closed my eyes and tuned into Sheba. "I did not care for gunfire and there was a reason for that. He is a good man who had forgotten to be respectful."

When I relayed this to Don he was surprised.

"Sheba changed me. I used to be quite the sportsman. I would kill just for the fun of it. When Sheba came, she was so frightened by the gunfire that I quit hunting. It changed my perspective on killing just for the fun. I don't have a problem with people hunting for food, but I do think it's wrong to hunt just for a trophy."

Sheba went on to share more about the seventeen years she had lived with this man. She showed me images of riding in a truck, the rush of the wind blowing her floppy ears back.

"I bought that truck for her," Don added. "She went just about everywhere with me."

Don and Sheba shared memories of their adventures together. I was told about their trips to the lake and the boat rides that were any Lab's fantasy. If they were not going somewhere, then they were together at home. Never was she far from his side. She communicated the contentment and joy of companionship at it finest.

Now that she was no longer with Don in physical form, she still expressed her love for him. She requested that I give him a message that he might keep in remembrance of her and to answer any questions that he might have.

"My beloved Friend,

The backfiring of the motorcycle did not cause me to leave. I used it as an excuse. It was time for me to go, and I took the opportunity. I could not bear to bring you more pain by allowing you to see me die. I love you more than words can come close to saying. My decision to go was not an easy one because I knew the pain it would cause you; however, I knew it was my time. I had grown accustomed to my physical pain, but my body was just worn out. I had done what I had come to do in this lifetime. I chose the woods because it is a good place to die. I was at peace in the woods and so it seemed fitting that I go there to leave my physical body behind.

"Enough of my physical death. I want you to remember the joys and lessons of our friendship. I enjoyed life. I feel it was lived to the fullest. I loved the wind in my face, the sun on my body, playing with you, but mostly I enjoyed just being with you, at your feet or by your side. . . . I came to you because I knew your heart and it is good. One with a good heart is rewarded from the heavens. The Father above rewarded us both by bringing us together. When you think of me, I am there; when you need me, I am there; when the time is right I will return in physical form to live with you again."

—Sheba, a dog, through Patty Summers

As a minister's daughter, I was taught to believe in a heaven. As far as I was concerned, heaven was not exclusive to humans. Animals went there as well. For without animals it would not be heaven. When I was a child, animals that had passed on would usually visit me in my dreams to let me know they were okay. When my father, and later my younger sister, passed into spirit, they too came to me to let me know all was well. I realize how blessed I am to experience the peace and joy that they feel in this place. It is simply indescribable. If there was one thing I could give a person whose animal had passed or was soon to pass into spirit, it would be to experience the love and peace of those in the spirit world.

When I was still at the animal shelter there was a little kitten. She was around eight weeks old, a gray and black tabby. Her eyes, which should have been wide with innocence and curiosity, were matted almost completely shut. Her nose was caked with dried discharge and her legs could no longer support her frail little body. She was dying.

"This is just awful," said the woman who found the kitten by a dumpster. "Someone must have left her there to die."

I gazed at the small furry being lying on the towel in the cardboard box. "Thanks for bringing her in," I said.

Euthanasia was the humane thing to do. I knew that, as I watched her struggle for each breath.

She left quickly, from gentle hands. "Someone needs to mourn for her," I thought. As I wiped the tears from my eyes, a vision appeared to me. I saw a group of female beings in human-like form. They appeared to be angelic girls between the ages of six and twelve, each wearing some sort of light-colored gown. Each seemed to sparkle and exude light. Smiling and giggling, they were reaching out to something at their feet. The kitten ran toward them healthy and radiant. One of the girls/angels picked up the kitten and cuddled her as the others moved close to stroke her as well. I could hear purring and the words, "No need to mourn. She is with us now."

The gift of the vision reminded me to take a look at what I really was grieving. It was not the kitten's passing, but humanity's lack of respect for beings like this one.

Distinguishing my pain from another's has been invaluable to me. A woman called me concerning her cat friend Tuser. Tuser's person called me because of Tuser's recurring cancer. "We wish to get her input as to how she wants us to proceed with this," she said. "Another surgery is an option, but the doctor's prognosis is not good and we do not wish to put her through any more than we have to."

"I understand," I replied.

I tuned into the gray calico with the white socks and bib. Her beautiful green eyes reflected warmth and wisdom, yet I could also sense her warrior-like energy. She carried herself in confidence, love, and joy. When I asked Tuser about having another surgery, she told me there was no need, as the cancer would only return. "I am at peace with my destiny; please find peace as well," she told her people. When I asked her if her people could do anything for her, she replied, "Look at me. Do I wallow in self pity? Do I appear depressed? Do not confuse your pain for mine. I know you must grieve. Do so. I respect your needs. . . . You know I am fulfilled. You feel this inside. . . ."

Tuser did not have the surgery. She remained with her people for months before she passed on into spirit. From the spirit world she told her people, "Oh, my life was good. I am in gratitude for a life well lived. I have known and know love, enjoyed a graceful and strong body, and shared."

For me, I have taken her words, "Do not confuse your pain with mine," and applied them to my interaction with all of my brothers and sisters. To own what is my pain, rather than projecting it onto another, enhances all of my communications.

For clients who are faced with a dying animal, or one with a chronic disease, the ability to separate their feelings from the animal's becomes most difficult. Some will go to any length to spare an animal friend's life. Unfortunately the lengths that some people go to in order to keep their friend alive is more for the person than the animal. They have confused their pain with the animal's. In almost all of the consults I do concerning dying animals, the animals ask me to relay to their people that they want their humans to make peace with their dying. They want their people to know that this is not an ending, only a change. So far I have never met an animal that feared death.

A young male cat was diagnosed with a fatal disease with no known cure. What he shared with his people reflects many animals' perspectives on living.

> *"The knowledge that I have a defined disease does not concern me. I am here now and I have this life to experience and all it has to offer. I have a strong desire to live life to its fullest. I do not feel sorry for myself. I am a beautiful and regal being with people who recognize this. The emphasis needs to be on my life and what I can do while I am here. At some point all must give up their physical existence and this does not frighten or sadden me. To die is simply a part of the life experience. We do not measure our lives with time. Quality in life is what is important. I came to remind you of the importance of living in the now."*

—A cat, through Patty Summers

Love that is beyond words and that transcends all boundaries. Love that is unmistakable and without conditions. This is what our animal brothers and sisters offer us. A woman once contacted me because she still grieved for her dog. Smokey conveyed transcending love to her, which is applicable to anyone who has known the love of a companion now in spirit.

"Gentle is my presence. I am never far. I will not leave you. I shall stand near you always. Feel the softness of the wings of my support. My role in your life has not changed, my form has. The light of my love has not been extinguished, only made more expansive.

"It is time to release your mourning and experience the unceasing love between us. Let the joy of love heal your saddened heart."

—Smokey, a dog, through Patty Summers

DUSTY, IS THAT YOU?

"Has Clairol been a dog of mine in a previous life?" Lindy asked. It is a question I hear fairly often. I directed the question to the setter. Clairol showed me an image of another setter, similar in appearance to her current physical form. Then came the image of being run over by a vehicle. "She says she was another setter who was hit and killed," I answered. Tears welled in Lindy's brown eyes.

"So how come animals remember their past lives so easily?" a woman asked me. I believe it has to do with the purity of animals' spiritual connections. Animals do not live in a society that puts emphasis on scientific proof for validity. Most have not alienated themselves from the inner knowledge of universal truth.

For most of my adult life I have struggled with my mainstream background in animal training and the more spiritual aspect of my animal communication work. Before going into animal communication work full time, I had worked at several veterinary practices, managed several pet supply stores, was an animal control officer, owned and operated my own pet-sitting business, and was the assistant manager of a humane society. I shared my animal communication abilities with hardly anyone. There were times when I felt in great conflict, and it was not until the last few years of my former employment that I was comfortable talking about my animal communication abilities. Reincarnation was a topic that I found especially uncomfortable to discuss. "Besides," I thought, "although past-life information is interesting and at times helpful, too much emphasis is often given to the past."

Lindy began to share with me about her former dog. Clare was run over while Lindy was out of town visiting her grandmother, who was undergoing bypass surgery, and her mother, who was suffering from bone cancer. When Lindy received the news that her beloved dog had been killed, she cried and cried. "Life seemed so unfair," she said. "I was having a horrible time dealing with my mother's illness, and now my Clare was dead."

Clare had been born on July 19. Clairol was born on July 14, one year later. "Clairol picked me out fairly quickly. I debated on a name for a long time," Lindy told me. "Clare kept coming to mind, but I had never named an animal the same as a previous animal. Six weeks went by. Then a friend of the family brought over his foster daughter to see the puppies. The young girl walked up to the puppy, looked into her face and said, "You must name this puppy Miss Clairol, as she already has her makeup on."

During another visit to Lindy's, we were discussing how animals come to us for a particular reason: to help us learn something, or vice versa. Lindy said to me, "Clairol has taught me that we do have second chances, and perhaps this time around in life is only a moment in the bigger scheme of things. She was my support and strength through my mother's painful struggle with cancer and my emotional roller coaster. Clairol has given me faith in death and the ever-after." I smiled inwardly. Lindy had brought to light the importance of the reincarnation aspect I had not fully acknowledged before.

A friend called me one morning concerning her elderly dog. Gordie, a golden retriever who now was more white than golden, was born with many physical challenges. He had not been expected to live a full life, and his original person had planned on euthanizing the pup. Chris, my friend, is a veterinary technician and was working at the animal hospital where the pup had been taken to be put to sleep. It was love at first sight, and she asked if she could adopt the little golden. The pup was hydrocephalic (a disease causing abnormal amounts of fluid in the skull) and later was diagnosed with hip dysplasia (a degenerative disease of the hips). His quality of life had been in question, yet in Chris's care the dog not only had a quality life, he had a long one, living to twelve years old.

Gordie loved going on walks and playing with his dog companions. He even indulged in the favorite sport of retrievers, swimming. He was not quite as fast or graceful as his dog friends, but his courageous heart more than made up for that. His enthusiasm and willingness made him endearing and easy to live with, despite his challenges.

At twelve years old, Gordie found that walking was becoming more of an effort. Finally, getting up—much less walking—was something Gordie could no longer do. Chris called me to confirm what she already knew. "I'm sure he is ready," she said. "I just want to know where he would like to be put to sleep. I can make arrangements to let him go here in his backyard if he'd like," she said.

"He says he can think of no better place to die than in his backyard, with you by his side," I answered.

Chris, believing in reincarnation, asked if Gordie would someday return to her in physical form. He answered that he would.

With the sun on his back, the soft earth under his body, and his dear friend by his side, Gordie left his worn-out body. It was because of the love of this woman that Gordie had the opportunity to experience the full life cycle from puppyhood to adulthood to a ripe old age. Gordie seized the opportunity and showed us that life is what you make of it, no matter what challenges you might face.

It was morning, approximately two years later. The phone rang. "Patty, you are not going to believe what happened this morning." It was Chris.

"What?" I asked.

"I woke up this morning feeling like something special was going to happen. I went out to feed the dogs and there was this tiny black puppy trying to get into the dogs' fenced-in area."

"That's wild," I said.

"Yeah, I thought so too. When I picked her up I had the funniest feeling that Gordie was no longer in the spirit world. Would you check and see if I'm right," she asked.

Gordie had returned as this small black furry pup. Little Bear, the pup, said a man had dropped her off at the edge of the road near where Chris lived. At first she was bewildered as the car drove off and she was left standing on the side of the road. What was she to do next? Where was her Mother Dog? Then came the barking. She stopped and perked her tiny ears to hear more clearly. A distant memory stirred; the barking was familiar. Her tiny legs ran as fast as they could, carrying her in the direction of the barks.

"She was like a little peg who had been left out and now fits right in," said Chris.

Once, while I was driving through town, something caught my eye. "What is that?" I said to my friend who was riding with me.

"I think it was a dog," she answered.

"I hope not; it looked more like a stick figure. Let's go back," I said and made a U-turn. He stood near a bridge that supported a four-lane highway. I blinked hard, not believing my eyes. The stick figure ran off down an embankment and under the bridge. My friend and I hopped out of my vehicle. I asked the friend to stay with the car while I walked down the steep embankment.

As I reached the bridge, I noticed dozens of empty liquor bottles. Realizing I had just walked into someone's hangout, I became very wary. I suppose the bridge provided cover for all kinds. Luckily I did not have to go far. I spotted the walking black and tan skeleton about thirty feet from me. He wore a leather collar that was three times too big for him; connected to the collar was a chain leash. I crouched down and began speaking softly to the animal, which was some sort of a hound. "Hi," I said. "I only want to help. I can feel you do not trust me.

That's understandable. Please relax enough to feel my true intentions." The dog softened, but still would not approach me. Then I remembered the french fries in my car. I called to my friend to get them for me.

I put the fries down on the ground and backed away. The dog was eager to eat. As he looked up at me, I noticed his sweet eyes. There was also something familiar in those eyes. I knew I had to help him. "I promise that if you will trust me I will find you a good home where you will never again go hungry," I told him. I could grab his leash, I told myself; however, if he decided to pull away he would easily slip out of that loose collar. I pondered a moment and decided to take a chance. The leash lay beside him, just within my grasp, as he ate the fries. I seized the opportunity. I had read him right. He did not struggle. Gently I picked him up and carried him to my car.

I was amazed at how well behaved he was in the car and how comfortable he seemed to be with me. Closer inspection of his collar showed a rabies tag. This in turn yielded the number of his former people. I was prepared to give them what for. I never got the chance. They never returned any messages concerning the dog. Further investigation informed me that the hound's former people had been in trouble with the animal warden before. I was grateful that they made no effort to retrieve him.

I asked the dog if he wished to go back to his people. He showed me a skinny man yelling at him. The man towered over the dog. He found them very confusing and angry people. He communicated to me that he had been on a walk with this man when he got loose. He thought it was great fun to run around free, as he normally was chained. The man did not think it was funny and yelled at the dog. When the dog noticed the man turn and begin to walk away, he followed. Suddenly something was whirled at him and it made a cracking noise as it hit the ground near him. The man began yelling at the dog again. The hound could sense that the man's anger was much greater. Fearing for his life, he ran in the opposite direction. Before long he found himself near a river.

He thought about going home only when his hunger got the better of him. Now, being hungry was a part of life that he had grown accustomed to. He survived by eating what he found along the river and road, trash and other items that I would rather not guess at. He shared images of people coming at night to sit under his bridge. They would drink from bottles and then often threw the bottles at him.

I brought him home without my usual introductions beforehand, something that I now realize was odd. I had told my animal family that he was coming until I could find him a home, but I did not tell the hound anything about my animals.

It was quickly apparent that he was a free spirit. We have a fenced area for our dogs so that, unless my husband or I am with them, they do not run loose. Ezra, as we now called him, would not be contained. He simply jumped the fence as if he were part deer. There was something in his run, in the exhilaration in his eyes; a distant memory lit up in my mind. Ever so lightly; not enough for full illumination, yet.

Although Ezra held no social skills to speak of, there was something endearing about the dog. Perhaps it was his great enthusiasm as well as his persistence. Perhaps it was his lease on life. He jumped into everything with joy. He was so happy to be here. His lack of social skills made his stay with our family difficult at times. He just did not know when to stop trying to make the others like him or accept him.

The biggest problem we had with Ezra was the way he responded to the goats. One look at them and he was off running, totally engaged in the chase. I was horrified. Somehow I was able to catch him before he caught a goat. I scolded him as he looked at me in confusion. He did not understand why he could not chase the goats. We decided to restrict Ezra's freedom while the goats were loose. It was inconvenient, but it was only temporary until we found the dog a good home.

In the weeks ahead I put up flyers and informed friends of Ezra's search for a home. A month went by, then another. What was the problem? Why could I not find him a good home? Deep inside I heard, "There is more to him than you have come to know." We decided to see if we could get Ezra to understand that the goats were part of the family and must be treated with respect. I looked deeper into his eyes in an attempt to communicate the importance of my message. Then there was full illumination of that distant memory.

It all made sense now. This was why I'd had so much trouble finding Ezra a home. The background was similar: Enduring cruelty while living on the streets of the inner city. The wildness of his spirit and that fierce look in his eyes when on guard. The desire to be a free spirit. The trust in me, even with his past human experiences.

"You've cut your hair," I joked. "You look nothing like you did before, except those eyes. I can't believe you're back, Dusty. I am afraid you have not learned your lesson from your last time around, concerning the goats."

"I have no desire to kill them as before, but I cannot give up the chase," came the response.

I shook my head. "Chasing them is not acceptable either. We are going to have to work on that habit if you are going to remain here. In the meantime, welcome back, friend."

MAKING PEACE

Her name was Happy.
How ironic, I thought.
This was one of the most miserable cats I had ever met. Names can be very important, due to the connotations behind them. I wondered why Happy's name did not influence her lease on life.

"Her name is kind of a joke," said Ann, the cat's person. "We have had Happy since she was a newborn kitten. Her mother cat disappeared one day, and my family and I ended up raising her and her three littermates. The other kittens adjusted well. Happy has always appeared miserable."

Ann had called me because of Happy's undesirable toilet habits. She was at her wit's end. "At first," she said, "I thought that at fifteen, her health was affecting her behavior, so I took her to the veterinarian and that has been ruled out. Happy does have health problems, but the doctor says they are not related to her toilet habits. Due to her other health problems, and now this, I get the feeling that she wants to die."

"Okay," I said, "let's see what she has to say about it."

As I tuned into the shorthaired gray cat, I was overcome with feelings of embitterment. Anger toward Ann, resentment toward life. "I am sorry that this is something you are experiencing," I communicated. I sensed that her resentment was largely due to her mother "abandoning" her and the other kittens. The other three kittens had adapted quickly to their mother's absence. Happy felt the crush of abandonment and still carried resentment in her heart.

"Happy said that she felt she had to take on responsibility for the other kittens. This was her way of dealing with the pain of her mother leaving them," I told Ann.

"That is strange," Ann said. "I always felt that Tommy, the male kitten, took care of the other kittens."

"He could have; Happy did not want the responsibility, yet she felt it was her duty—" I stopped as Ann interrupted.

"Wait a minute," she said with astonishment, "I remember now finding tiny wet spots on Happy's tummy where the others had suckled her. Tommy seemed to be the emotional stability for the others, but I guess Happy was the physical caregiver—at first, anyway."

"It's not so different from humans. I can think of many people who take on certain roles and act them out physically, yet their heart is not in that role," I replied. "Resentment is bound to occur."

I acknowledged Happy's emotional pain. "That must have been hard," I communicated. "You were blessed to have had a person who helped you nurture your cat family." She softened for a moment but then stiffened with anger. "Why are you angry with Ann?" I asked. It turned out that Happy was angry about the way Ann had handled the death of Tiger, a littermate. Tiger had been put to sleep recently, due to chronic health reasons. Happy felt she was not made a part of what was going on with Tiger.

"Well," Ann said, "that is true. I did not even think about talking to the other cats about Tiger. I simply took her to the veterinarian, and after she was euthanized I left her body there. I thought they knew she was very sick."

"Yes, they knew," I answered. "It is not so much that she was put to sleep as it is that Happy felt that you did not think her feelings mattered or that you did not even acknowledge that she was sad, too."

"She's right," Ann replied. "The way Happy acts, I did not think she cared that much."

I explained to Ann that destructive or undesirable behavior that develops is usually a way for the animal to communicate that something is wrong. When a veterinarian rules out health concerns, then the animal's person needs to look at what could have changed, upsetting the animal. Animals normally do not just go around trying to make our lives miserable by using our rugs for toilets or chewing up our furniture. The animal is usually saying, "Hey, I'm bored or frustrated." In Happy's case her bad toilet habits were her way of saying, "I'm pissed off," or "I'm angry." Animals will find a way to communicate their feelings.

Happy's anger gave way to sadness. Tiger was the baby, in her eyes. "You were a good sister to her," I told the cat. "Yes, I will join her soon," she replied. "So you do wish to pass into spirit?" I asked. "Soon but not quite yet," she answered. I shared all of this information with Ann.

"What do I do now?" Ann asked.

"It is time for you to sit with Happy and acknowledge her feelings concerning Tiger," I answered.

"I feel terrible that I did not do this earlier," she said.

"You were not aware at the time," I said. "Now you are. That's all you need to say from your heart. Now is the time for Happy to make peace with her life, and you are the one to help her."

Ann did what I suggested with delightful results. Not only did Happy return to more acceptable toilet habits, she appeared to be, well, happy. Approximately one month later Ann called me. The cat had quit eating and was going downhill fast. "Is it time now?" Ann asked. A peaceful Happy said she would be leaving soon.

> *"When my cat mother told me she would not be returning, I wanted to die. As you know, I became embittered and resentful, mostly at the Universe for dealing me such an unfair life. . . . All my life I immersed myself in the muck and mire of anger. Tiger's death was a turning point. Did I wish to leave this world with a hostile heart? Knowing I wanted to make peace within myself, I turned to the one who showed me love, despite my unlovable behavior. It was there that I found the help I sought. You've empowered me to achieve inner peace...."*

> —Happy, a cat, through Patty Summers

A few days later, in her home, while laying on the lap of Ann's daughter, Happy left this plane of existence.

CIRCLE
OF LOVE

Early on in my animal communication work, I was discussing with a friend I had not seen in a year some of what the animals had shared. It was a beautiful summer's day as we sat on my front deck enjoying the view of the mountains. We had much to catch up on. Both of us had moved into new homes and locations and both were excited about the changes in our lives.

"Since I have decided to do my communication work as a business I feel truly blessed," I said. "The more communication work I do, the more I feel I receive spiritual growth."

"Interesting," my friend said.

I continued to share excitedly how I had come to know and understand love more deeply than ever.

As I chatted away I noticed that Ereenie, my oldest female cat, had joined us. I smiled at her. "Ereenie has taught me love at its finest." I went on a bit more before it became obvious to me that my friend was not listening. I stopped talking, realizing that my words were falling on deaf ears.

My friend took a deep breath and said, "Patty, Ereenie is a lovely being, but she is a cat. She is not as evolved as we humans; therefore, some of what you are sharing is not possible for her."

I felt a knife had been shoved in my heart. This was my friend, or at least I had thought so. In the past we'd had countless discussions on metaphysical subjects. I knew she believed in telepathic communication. Now I found that she believed in it as long as it supported her belief in human superiority.

Quickly I masked my pain with anger toward her. I sat quietly after she changed the subject. I felt fur against my leg and knew Ereenie had come to lend me support, as she normally did in times of emotional pain. I leaned over to pick her up, but she kept going, stopping in front of my friend. "Meeeooooow," she said as she positioned herself at the woman's feet.

"Come on up, Ereenie," my friend said.

Ereenie jumped on her lap and began purring. As my friend continued telling me her thoughts I stared at Ereenie, astonished at her display of what I felt was betrayal of me.

I looked into the dark brown tabby's green eyes and communicated. "Just what are you doing? Did you hear her just a minute ago? She was belittling you."

"My dear Patty," came her soft and loving "voice," "pay attention to what this woman is really communicating. To hear that a mere animal has taught you of love threatens her spiritual teachings. She is in fear. She does not need my anger, for this is not about me. She needs my love." Ereenie, whose name means peace, once again lived up to her name.

I did what Ereenie suggested, deciding to allow this woman her perspective. After all, I had nothing to prove. I was the student with a continual lesson of looking deeper at what was really being communicated, a human experiencing the meaning of unconditional love from its greatest teachers. The animals share that love is a circle, making all whole and complete — the understanding that we all are a part of one another, and that in giving to one, we give to one another.

A woman called me concerning her deceased dog, Gee. She carried much guilt in her heart because he had died of a prolonged illness. "I just wonder if he is mad at us or if he felt we did all we could for him," she said. In the photo she had sent me was a woman with a little tan Pekinese perched on her lap. His feathered tail plumed out as he held it high in joy.

"It appears he was a joyful dog," I said.

"His life was sad at first," said the woman. "He used to live with an older woman who was a friend of ours. She passed away when Gee was around a year old. That's something I'd like to know too: if he missed her."

She went on to tell me that Gee appeared to fit right into her family. "At first he was a little depressed, but he seemed to get over that fairly quickly. We knew him when he lived with our friend, so I think that helped in his transition."

When I tuned into Gee he was grateful for the opportunity to communicate to these people. He knew of their pain and wished to offer comfort.

> *"I hope that I did not leave your hearts empty, for you have filled mine. I did not doubt in your care for me. So why would you question yourselves? You showed me that love always exists. Love never dies. You were my teachers in this. You welcomed me as part of your family. What I offer you is the lesson I have come to learn: Love is a continual circle. Her (his former person's) love for me continued through you. I was able to share with you the love in my heart. You would honor me by allowing your love for me and mine for you, to continue by sharing it with another. Love makes us complete. It is not who we share it with, but that we share it."*

—Gee, a dog, through Patty Summers

The circle of love continued on when a yellow Lab named Biscuit left her person, Paula. Paula was a young woman who had attended one of my workshops on animal communication. During a break Paula asked me if I could communicate with an animal who had been gone for years.

"Yes," I answered, "life goes on, maybe not in the same form, yet that being still exists."

"Well about four years ago my dear Lab, Biscuit, disappeared. Our housekeeper let her out and she never returned. It was heartbreaking, never knowing what happened to her, and I feel I need some closure," Paula said.

The consult revealed Biscuit to be a delightful, youthful being. She told me that when she was let out of her home she caught the smell of something. She followed that smell down the driveway. Then, seeing something across a rural road, she headed in that direction. She had a blast satisfying her curiosity; however, she also knew that she was off to the next phase of her life's journey.

Shortly thereafter she found herself in the middle of a two-lane highway. Cars beeped and swerved around the unconcerned dog. Finally he arrived, the man that Biscuit would go home with. His car came to a halt and he got out to offer Biscuit safety in his car. She hopped inside happily. She went on to show me the man taking her to a building with other people.

The man carried something that looked like a briefcase. She watched him talk a bit with some of these people. He then pointed at Biscuit, and several of the people petted her. She said the man was telling them about how he found her in the road.

After a time, the man had her jump back into his car and he drove to the location where he'd found her. There he pulled off into driveways and got out, knocking on doors. Sometimes, Biscuit relayed, he took her with him up to the house; sometimes he just pointed to her in the car. He was trying to find where she lived. Biscuit said she waited patiently. She knew she was where she belonged now.

"I am happy to share with you finally, so that you will know all is well. . . . Of course I loved you, but I was needed elsewhere. . . . Please do not be angry with this man. He made an effort to reunite me with you," Biscuit shared.

They made numerous stops at people's homes. Biscuit said they rode in the car for a long time. Eventually she arrived at her new home. She showed me a little boy who had some sort of handicap. I was unsure what his challenge was. Biscuit said, "He was special and I had come to help. To his parents I took care of the child. In reality he (the child) was a higher being. I came to be his companion and to give his human parents comfort."

Biscuit went on to tell me that the child had since died and now she aided in relieving the emotional suffering of the parents.

She was still in physical body and doing well. "I know I have served them well and they have loved me dearly," she added. "As for you, I know I made you happy when I was with you. I loved to hear you laugh. Your heart got heavy sometimes. It was good to see it lighten. I know you feel we were not together long, but it was quality time. I have sent you messages that I was okay. You have remained in my heart and I send you love often. Please do not blame others for my leaving. It was meant to be. It was not that I love my present people more, just that at this time I was destined to serve them. My love for you can never be replaced or weakened by anything or anybody."

I had written all of this information down for Paula to keep. I handed it to her and waited in case she had questions. She looked up from the sheet of paper that recorded the consult; tears were streaming down her pretty face. I hoped that I was able to express the love Biscuit had for Paula. I walked away to get Paula some tissues. She wiped her tears and looked off in the distance in deep thought. Wishing to respect her privacy, I excused myself and told her where she could find me if she had questions.

A few minutes later I felt a hand on my arm. "Patty, it's my turn to share the rest of Biscuit's and my story. You see, I tried to commit suicide. It was Biscuit who saved me. When she is talking about my heart being heavy at times, well, she was right. It was the joy that Biscuit gave me that pulled me through a very difficult time in my life. She lived with me for only two years and I did feel cheated, but I also must admit that when she left I was much stronger. I was full of hatred toward our housekeeper for letting Biscuit outside that day. I realize now that I need to forgive her. I also need to tell you that Biscuit had been trained to be a service dog for the handicapped. I have felt that all along she was still alive."

There was peace in Paula's bloodshot eyes. A soft smile began to light up her face. A tear of joy fell from my eye.

There are times when the circle of love continues through the help of what some would call a guardian angel. Yes, animals can have guardian angels as well. You never know who that guardian angel might be.

Maria was driving down the highway on her way to work on a bright autumn day, when she saw something white on the side of the road. She pulled onto the shoulder of the bypass and backed up directly across from a dog. "I just knew he had been hit. When I got to him I could see the red on his face, blood. He couldn't stand up, both front legs were fractured and he had some broken teeth. Anyway the doctor says he'll be okay. Meanwhile I wondered if you could help me figure out what happened and where he came from," she said to me.

I smiled at the setter mix sitting in the back seat of my friend's car. His long white hair was accented with a few black spots on his body and a large black ring around one eye. "He's quite handsome," I said partly to Maria and partly to the dog. I quieted myself and began to tune into him. He showed me a flash of silver-colored metal. For a moment I was in his body, feeling myself whirling through the air. "A fender," I thought. "You already knew he was hit; the car sent him sailing. I'm surprised he survived," I shared with Maria.

"Where are you from?" I communicated to the dog. He showed me a family and a home in a country setting. The dog said he lived a carefree life. He ran free and went home when he was hungry. His people were not cruel in the sense of physically abusing him, but there was little interaction with the dog. "They have no interest in me. This is where I would like to be for now," he said. "I was dissatisfied with my people. I wanted more. I did not intend on getting injured, but it is a means to an end. . . ." I frowned at him, a bit puzzled. He continued, "She told me to wait here. Help would come." He shared an image of a brown dog. The dog was not physically present; she was in spirit. Light shimmered around her as she appeared near him. His guardian angel had told him that help was on the way.

As I relayed all of this information to Maria, the brown dog revealed who she was.

"Oh, my Lord," I gasped.

"What?" Maria asked.

"It's Coyote, your former dog," I answered.

"Oh Patty," Maria said, "when I found him I kept feeling Coyote's presence. I wondered if he was her, come back. To top this off, I'm telling you it was weird. He was just patiently lying there along the road, head up as if he were waiting for a taxi. I thought it was so strange that a dog who had been hit would be so calm. He wasn't in shock, just calm as if he knew all would be okay. Now I know why," she added.

Maria decided to call him "Boo," because he reminded her of a ghost with his white body and black markings. Although Maria loved Boo, she had a road trip planned that would consume nearly a year of her life and take her across the seas. She felt this was no life for the dog, so she found him a home out in the country with a lovely woman who wanted a companion for her Lab.

Although the woman provided Boo a good and loving home, he never completely bonded to her. Maria's parents lived in the same town that Boo lived in, so in between journeys, Maria would stop to visit her parents and Boo. It never failed that, when Maria would call to check on the dog, that his caregiver would say, "I knew you were in town. Boo's been sitting in the front yard closely examining every car to see if it is you." It became apparent that Boo had decided his place was at Maria's side. Once Maria's travels were over, she returned and made Boo a part of her family, completing a circle of love.

Walking in Balance and Harmony

My hus-
band and I
were so happy
to move into our new home. We felt fortunate to be the
caretakers of a lovely piece of property. Our home is surrounded
by woods, with a grand view of the mountains from our front
deck. I knew our animal family would be very happy there as
well. It was a great place to take my dogs for walks, and the
cats had plenty of room to roam safely. There was also room
for more animals, as I knew more would come in the future,
such as Ms. Goat and her family. It was our first springtime at
the new home. Two of our cats began doing their version of a

Lewis and Clark expedition, exploring their new country. Ereenie was content to be queen of the indoors, where nothing went on without her scrupulous watch. Her furry body adorned every lap and piece of furniture at some point or another. She would occasionally take a stroll outside for some fresh air, but she was a cat who enjoyed the comforts of home.

Her twin brother Freeman was exactly the opposite. He loved the outdoors and assumed the role of marshal of the land. No animal could set foot on his land without going through him first. He would patrol the land with vigilance. If trouble could not be found on his property, then he'd go out and find some. There was always someone somewhere who needed straightening out.

To me, Squeaky resembles a princess. She is graceful and beautiful with long white hair, tabby spots, and big green eyes. Her pink nose sets off her ladylike appearance. But her outside appearance betrays the inner cat. Inside lives a great huntress. I will not go into detail, but the variety of game that she caught was enough to prove that the cat's hunting abilities are great.

I can remember once rounding the corner of my kitchen to enter the living room and finding Squeaky wrapped around something green. My heart was in my throat when I realized that what Squeak had her arms wrapped around was the bird. I screamed, "Squeaky what do you think you are doing?" When they unlocked, I discovered that it was an embrace. Looking up at me in bewilderment, they both asked me what was wrong. I was astonished to find that Squeaky the huntress had become bosom buddies with a bird. I knew Popagolis was quite taken with her. "She is beautiful," he would say. Up until that day, Squeak had pretty much ignored him. From that point on Popagolis decided Squeaky was his mate. It was common to find them sitting together, often with him preening her head.

I respect Squeaky's instincts. I ask only that she maintain balance, keeping in mind that I provide her with food. If she feels the need to make a kill, then she is expected to consume the one whose life she takes. Squeaky pretty much held up her end of the bargain. But last spring she went on what I felt was a wild rampage. She had thought she entered a huntress's paradise, with wildlife galore. It became a daily routine for Squeak to return from the outdoors with a lifeless baby rabbit in her mouth. One day she came in with one and consumed it, and later that day I found her with yet another soft brown baby. I knew I had to intervene. "Squeaky, I have to remind you that this is not balance. You are taking more than you need," I communicated. She paused, thinking over my words, and communicated that she would curb her instincts. I was relieved to find in the next few weeks that she respected my wishes.

People ask me if there is a difference between communicating with wild animals and communicating with domestic ones.

I have observed that beings in the wild retain their sense of balance with all. Sometimes the domestics, through their association with humans, forget that sense of balance.

Squeaky's hunting rampage is one example of this. Shortly after I had my "talk" with Squeak, I was standing outside doing a meditative exercise when I noticed a rabbit in the front yard watching me with curiosity. I tuned in to receive her communication. "What are you doing?' came the thought. "It is a form of exercise to relax my mind and strengthen my body," I answered. "Interesting," communicated the rabbit. I sensed she was a female and wondered if she could be the mother rabbit of the babies Squeak had consumed. "I am," came the reply from the gentle being. Guilt overcame me as I apologized to her. "We moved onto this property that you had already made your home. I feel I have allowed my family member to invade you. I am so sorry."

"There is no need to be sorry. Yes, I loved my children, and I understand the circle of life. I felt a loss and I know that all die and at some point all will give their bodies to nurture another, whether it be our Mother (Earth) or another being who shares the earth."

As she nibbled on the clover in the yard I felt the inner peace her knowledge gave her. What she had shared became clear. The vegetation gave of itself to sustain her and at some point she would either be consumed by a predator, helping to sustain its body, or die of natural causes, in which case her body would nurture the earth. I heard words, the origins of which I was not sure: "The key is respect and honor for all of life. Walk in balance and harmony with all your relations."

A few days after my encounter with the rabbit I looked out the window and to my astonishment saw Squeaky sitting within six feet of a rabbit. Squeaky's posture made it obvious that she was not stalking the rabbit. She was just sitting there. The rabbit munched peacefully on the sweet clover, nose twitching, unconcerned about the cat nearby. Several years have passed and although Squeak still enjoys the thrill of the wild, it is rare that she makes a kill.

IT GOES BOTH WAYS

I have a bumper sticker on my car that reads, "Humans aren't the only species on the planet, we just act like it." The animals bring us back to our wholeness; they remind us that humanity is a part of that whole, not THE whole. There are times that I run across an animal that has grown weary of humans.

Domestic animals are usually more forgiving than wild ones, but still I have run across a few who wanted nothing to do with us humans. So it was with Carla the cow. Carla and her mother, Fanny, lived among a herd of beef cattle. A tenant on the farm property had adopted Carla's mother. Fanny lived among the herd and had become a beloved companion to the tenant, Jean. Jean called me because soon she would have to make a decision on what to do with the black and brown calf. The landlord of the farm allowed Jean to purchase Fanny, keeping the cow on the farm; however, his tolerance was thin. He saw the cows as profit and could not understand Jean's attachment.

Jean called me to get the calf's perspective. When I tuned into the calf, she communicated her dislike of humans. I was partly surprised, as I had found her mother to be quite friendly and amenable toward humans. Yet, with the disrespect cattle receive from humans, the attitude that should have surprised me was Fanny's. "I wish to remain with my herd, I do not want the companionship of a human," Carla responded. "This makes sense," Jean interjected. "She doesn't act like she likes people. She won't have anything to do with me when I go out to interact with Fanny. If she stays with the herd, does she understand that she will go to a feed lot to be fattened up and killed?" she added.

I communicated with Carla what her fate would be. She was already aware of it. There was no fear as she communicated back, "It is not death, but how I live my life that is important. I wish to remain with my kind." I relayed all of this to Jean.

"I can't believe this is what she wants," she said.

"Well, animals do usually look at quality verses quantity, and death is not a feared thing. Sure, they have survival instincts, but when death is inevitable they surrender, at peace with it. Carla is looking at the now, not the future," I said.

"This just makes me sad," Jean added.

"I understand where you're coming from. I also understand Carla's view of humanity and her desire," I said.

"If this is what she wants then I will honor it, but please tell her to think about it. We have a little time. I found an animal sanctuary for Fanny's first calf and perhaps they would take her too," Jean replied.

I communicated Jean's message to Carla.

A little over a month had passed when Jean called again. "Hi, Patty. I need you to check in with Carla again. The evening after you talked to her she walked up and stood near my husband and myself, watching us. It was rather strange. She still won't let me touch her, but she has never shown any interest at all in us."

"She says she finds you most curious," I told Jean. "She has never met a human like you. She wishes to tell you that she still wants to live with cattle. This is where she feels most comfortable. Since we last communicated with her she says her feelings toward humans have changed. 'Perhaps you are not all as you seem,' she said. She is quite impressed by the fact that you wished to know her desire for her life. She adds, 'I shall no longer view all humans in the same way.' Carla shares a sense of gratitude and respect toward you."

Softy Jean said, "Wow. I cannot believe I have an existential cow."

For Jean, the end to Carla's story is sad. Carla was stolen by the landlord of the farm and sold out of state. Attempts were made to locate Carla, with little success. All Jean was able to learn was that Carla was somewhere in the Midwest. Jean saw the dark side of humanity. Guilt weighed heavily on her shoulders, because she felt she had somehow forsaken Carla.

"Please tell her this is not what I had intended," Jean sobbed.

I closed my eyes and sent Jean's message to Carla. Somewhere in the Midwest there is a heifer who communicates to me a deep satisfaction. She thinks of a human who has touched her profoundly. Telling me her life has been changed. Even with disrespectful humans around her, she knows hope, for she says she witnessed the brighter side of humanity.

REPTILIAN WISDOM

Many wild animals have very poor opinions of us, with very good reason. They still remain at the banquet table our Mother Earth provides. They know that all their needs shall be provided and that there is no lack. They see themselves as part of the web, not as the spider. Balance and harmony is not a creed, it is a way of life. We, the two-legged humans, have journeyed away from that table. Believing in lack, we take more than we require, unconcerned about how our unbalance affects other life. We have alienated ourselves from our relations.

It was early fall when the animal warden found him lying cold and still on a suburban sidewalk. Surprised to find the dull green iguana was still alive, the warden transported the reptile to the local humane society. I had stopped by for a visit when I heard of Henry the iguana. Henry was now living with one of the staff members in her home.

"I can't believe people," I said. "They don't stop to think that these animals are not native to this country and that they can't be turned loose when they are tired of them." I was a little miffed.

"Well, he's doing much better now," Henry's caretaker told me.

A few weeks had passed when I got a phone call. "Patty, I can't keep Henry. He's started biting my family members. Do you want him?"

I paused. Since Popagolis had come to live with us, I had mixed feeling about exotic animals as house companions. The best place for the iguana was in a rainforest, but that was not realistic. I had always admired the iguana as a species and it felt like he was supposed to come live with us, so I said yes.

Henry's terror and disdain for humanity was great. Biting people, I was sure, was his way of expressing his feelings toward us. I am not sure which pain was worse, the pain in my heart from feeling his terror as I reached into his habitat to care for him, or the pain in my hands and arms after he whipped me with his tail. Iguanas must have been bullwhip experts in former lives. This reptile would keep me in his keen eye, waiting for the perfect positioning of my hand or arms; when they were in a place that gave him a clean shot he struck as hard and as quick as he could. I suppose I could consider myself lucky that he never attempted to bite me.

As I had shared with Ms. Goat when she first moved in, I told him that he was not here to be my pet. My family simply wished to give him as comfortable a home as possible. In time he did get more comfortable. Instead of whipping me five or six times when I reached into his living quarters, he whipped me only once or twice. He even requested a name change. He is now Henry Quasar Quantum, or Quasar for short.

Quasar's body grew into a beautiful shade of green, with blue markings. He also has tripled his body size. When he first came he wanted nothing to do with humans. He only tolerated me. I have grown quite fond of him and he has softened his heart toward humans. I have shared with him that he and I came together for a reason. He has made peace with living with my family and me. I know Quasar felt the respect I carried in my heart for him as my relative, and this is what helped him make his peace. I did not pity him, for I believe we all choose our paths. I showed him respect and honored who he was.

Talking with the Animals

Quasar now shares with others of my species.

"You have lost your way. Stop and listen—for you walk around disconnected from our Mother, wandering around grasping at false truths derived through human arrogance. You cannot hear, due to your own loud voices. STOP.

"Let the energy of life that connects us all flow. Breathe, feeling the energy rise up your spine, rooting, grounding you.

"We are not 'pets'; we are your brothers, your sisters. Only through respect can you gain ours. Only through coming home to your family, remembering who you and who we are, can you embrace wholeness."

—Quasar, an iguana, through Patty Summers

WE ARE ONE

The cream-colored tabby came to live with me when I was a teenager. We named him Ping-Pong. I cannot remember why we named him that; however, we helped him restore part of his dignity by more often calling him Mr. Pong. When Mr. Pong came into my life, I was sixteen and miserable.

My father, who had been diagnosed with Alzheimer's, was at a point where he needed more care than we could provide. His dementia was so advanced that he had become dangerous at times. There were frequent "escape" attempts from home, because he perceived us as strange people holding him captive. He would fight us violently when we stopped him. He was unable to make sane conversation, so the phone had to be guarded. We never knew whether he might stroll out of his room naked or bust out in a rage. I rarely had friends over to visit for this reason. At the time of my father's illness, little was known about Alzheimer's disease. This, coupled with the cruelty that young people can inflict when another does not fit into socially defined norms, left me socially handicapped. My mother finally made the painful decision to institutionalize him.

My father had to retire from the ministry because of this disease, and it seemed that things just got worse from that point on. Besides my father's illness, I also had a younger sister, Sandy, born with Down's syndrome and a defective heart. To me Sandy was a gift from the Universe. For all the health problems and emotional challenges, she brought much joy and wisdom. I adored her. The combination of Sandy's and my father's health issues brought many challenges into my life. Mental retardation was something people were familiar with, but still I felt the pain of judgment, if not toward me, then toward my sister or my family. By the time I reached sixteen I had decided that I pretty much hated people. Since I was technically a person, I extended those hostile feelings toward myself as well.

Throughout childhood I sought comfort from the animals. It seemed that only they could understand my pain, and it was only from them that I "felt" love. I knew my family loved me, yet I did not feel human love the way I felt love from the animals. Now that I was going through a dark stage in my life, this wonderful guardian came to me. It never failed that, should I find myself struggling emotionally, Mr. Pong the cat would appear out of nowhere. He would show up—sometimes asking to be petted, other times just sitting near or on me—remaining until I felt comforted. I could sense him sending love to me.

Ping-Pong was a source of much comfort for Sandy as well. With her he had the patience of a saint. He put up with many a tail pulling or a rough petting, never scratching or even hissing at her. Sandy suffered from chronic health problems. During the times she was bedridden, it was Mr. Pong who sat by her side. This earned him another title, "Nurse Ping-Pong." I remember a photo of this plump cat sitting on the bed next to Sandy. On his head was the tiny nurse's cap that my mother had made him. The expression on this good sport's face was, "Would you look at what I have to do to humor these people. Geez."

As a young adult and on my own, I had Ping living with me. After a year, he communicated that he had done what he had come to do for me, and that now he was needed elsewhere. Sandy and my now-widowed mother needed him. Even though my mom did not live that far from me, allowing me to visit when I liked, it was still hard to let him go. Ping-Pong had someone else who needed him more, and I could not allow my selfishness to interfere with that.

After that, he was "Nurse Ping" for about four more years. Sandy would call out for her nurse when she needed him. His service to her ended with him, my mother, and me by Sandy's side as she passed into the spirit world. Sandy's death was very hard on my family and myself. I was comforted to know that my mother was in good paws. There he remained until she was strong enough; then he too passed on to the spirit world.

My story is not unique. Page, my former coworker at the humane society, had a very special companion named Riley. Riley was a handsome yellow and orange longhaired tabby. When I met Riley I knew he, too, was a guardian. He exuded such peace and balance. He was sheer confidence without the ego. Page told me of how Riley had come to live with her and her family when he was a kitten. Page had two sons, and Riley became the older son's cat. Page suffered an abusive marriage to the father of her children, so her son's upbringing was less than harmonious. Page talked about Riley being a wonderful comforter, not only for her older son, but for all of the family. "He not only took care of us, but he also took care of the other animals that came to live with us," she said. "He got along with everyone."

When Riley died at the ripe age of seventeen, Page wrote his memoirs to give her son. She asked me to contact Riley and see what he wanted to add. As I listened I saw a young man upset and angry, while nearby a yellow and orange cat sits calmly with his eyes closed, concentrating as he sends unconditional love. As I read his message again, I see a young woman upset, crying, and angry at the world. Nearby is a cream-colored tabby, stout in stature. As he sits quietly intent on his task, the picture shifts to yet another young person and this time there is a dog sitting nearby, next an adult with a bird, and so on.

> *"Come walk with me and I shall show you things of my world. I lived at peace and in balance with all. I provided stability and a sense of the solid, yet I was not stagnant. I could go where I wished. One can be there for others and still maintain freedom of spirit. My strength came from my inner peace, my knowledge of the truth. I was a provider of comfort, yet I kept my center. I could not interfere with your journeys. Your path is your own, as was mine. My counsel was simply to listen and not judge or advise. I would, however, assist you in making your connection to the higher source when you requested it. All have access to the knowledge. It is the knowledge of the Universe, knowledge of the Ancient Ones. It is true that we are all one, all connected. We all have the ability to access the same knowledge. Know love never ceases. Love surrounds you. Remember how I walked through life. Come walk with me; I am your brother and my spirit carries on."*

—Riley, a cat, through Patty Summers

But ask the beasts, and they will teach you;
The birds of the air, and they will tell you;
Or the plants of the earth, and they will teach you;
And the fish in the sea will declare to you.
Who among all these does not know that the hand of the
    Lord has done this?
In his hand is the life of every living thing and the breath
    of mankind.

Job 12:7-10 (Holy Bible, Revised Standard Version)

REAWAKENING TO ANIMAL COMMUNICATION

I value my role as a bridge between humans and our animal brothers and sisters. The bridge leads to a table that exists for all of Mother Earth's children to sit at: the two-legged, the four-legged, the many-legged, those that burrow, those that fly, those that swim, those that crawl, the stone people and the plant people. While at this table all walk in balance and harmony. Even though some humans have forgotten the table exists, the invitation to return is always open.

Anyone can communicate with animals. It is the universal language, the thought or idea before the words. It is the gut feeling or inner knowing that some of us have. It is the picture that forms in our minds. Belief in our natural ability to communicate telepathically with animals is important. Acknowledging our ability is a big part of tuning into that frequency already available to us. We have been taught to ignore these types of communication, categorizing them as our imagination.

Along with the need to believe in our abilities comes the need for honesty, respect, mindfulness, and the knowledge that animals often have different perspectives than humans. We are all one family; each member of that family plays a different role. No role is less important. All are needed to make a whole.

Animals often complain to me that human thoughts are cluttered. We live in a fast-paced world. We tend to talk to our animals or human companions while doing or thinking about something else. This may work fine with a human who understands verbal language; however, when you give someone your full attention, you greatly enhance the chances for clarity in your communication.

Taking quiet time or centering ourselves brings us back into focus. Start practicing some meditation or just sit and take some deep, cleansing breaths. Breathe in through the nose and out through the mouth; inhale deeply into the abdomen, feeling the abdomen expand and contract. It is not necessary for you and your animal friend to look into each other's eyes. You may find it easier to focus or tune into your animal through closing your eyes. Or, you may want to gaze at the animal. Some people like to touch the animal. Experiment with what works best for you. Just bear in mind the importance of the animal's comfort as well. If the animal does not want to be touched, then do not touch him or her. Because this is telepathic communication, the animal does not even need to be physically present.

Once you have centered yourself and are able to give the animal your full attention, it is time to send what you wish to communicate. I recommend sending a picture from your mind's eye. Make your picture as clear as possible. Pretend you are speaking to someone with a foreign language. For example, say you want to teach your dog to sit and stay. You would get an image in your mind of the dog sitting and staying, and then mentally send that image to your dog or direct that thought to your dog. Think "sit" or say "sit" out loud or mentally. If you want to ask your dog a question such as, "How do you like your food?" visualize your dog at the food dish with the food that you normally serve. You can see yourself pouring it into the bowl and placing it in front of the dog. Then back it up with the thought, "How do you like this?"

If you are communicating with someone else's animal friend and are unsure how to picture something, ask for clarification. A person may call me and say, "Ask Sam what he thinks of Peanut." If I do not know who Peanut is, I cannot picture him in order to ask Sam the question.

I once was called to ask a Border collie what she thought of a new toy that her person Catherine had bought her. Story, the Border collie, was retired from the obedience ring due to an injury, so in an effort to keep Story mentally stimulated, Catherine had bought her what was called a Buster Cube. Catherine explained to me that it was a cube in which you put small bits of food or treats. The food then would fall into the maze inside the cube. The dog's job was to figure out which way to roll the cube in order to get the food out. I did not bother to ask Catherine what the toy looked like. I kept imaging this clear cube to Story, leaving her quite confused. Finally I asked what it looked like and it turned out that the cube was blue. The color was not so important; however, the image of a clear cube did not look at all like what Story knew, leaving Story to wonder what in the world I was talking about.

The next step is to relax, allowing your mind to go blank. Accept whatever communication you receive. If you asked how your dog likes his or her food, you may get a good feeling or a disgusted one. You may receive an image of your dog walking away from the bowl, or maybe you'll hear, "It's delicious." Take any judgments out of what you receive. Because most people have preconceived judgments concerning their personal animal friends, most people find it easier at first to communicate with someone else's animal friend.

Telepathic communication, as I mentioned earlier, is beyond verbal communication, so sometimes the communications may not make sense at first.

A couple called me to ask how their cat was physically. The cat said he was fine. The people told me that was incorrect, because the cat had a fatal disease. I explained to them that I asked the cat how he was feeling physically and he said, "fine." I then asked them if he was showing any physical signs of his illness. "Well, no, not yet. He went in for his check-up and when the test was run for this disease it came up positive," they answered.

You will get the animal's perspective or viewpoint. Keep this in mind. Just because someone may think he or she got an incorrect answer doesn't mean that it is so. If the response you receive does not make sense, then take a moment to examine that response. Is it interference from human judgment, or could it be that you just need to work on understanding communication from an animal's perspective?

If you do not receive anything, then try again later. If you receive an answer or response to something that is totally different from the question—say your dog gives you an image of chasing a ball—acknowledge that and ask the original question again. Sometimes the animal may wish to share something else that he or she finds more important.

Acknowledge any communication you make with an animal. If you were talking to another human, you would not conclude your question without acknowledgment. Neglecting to acknowledge the exchange is disrespectful. Would you feel like communicating further with someone who made no acknowledgment that the communication took place? Respect is the keynote in telepathic animal communication. An acknowledgment can come in the form of a word like "thanks," a mental or physical nod of the head, or a gentle stroke.

Okay, so now you are asking, "How do I know what I got is correct?" At first I would advise that you just have fun. Do not put pressure on yourself to get it right. In time you will learn to trust yourself, in addition to physical confirmation.

Say you asked your pet rabbit if he wanted anything special in his hutch. You visualize him inside his hutch and then see him looking around in it. You mentally ask, "Would you like something else in here?" Perhaps you visualize a carrot lying near him and then wait for his response. You get the idea that he wants a fresh piece of wood to chew on. It does not make a lot of sense, but what the heck, what can it hurt? You find him a freshly cut branch and put a piece of it inside his hutch. Later that day you notice he's chewed up the whole piece of wood and is asking for another.

Maybe you are at your friend's house and she is complaining about her bird's constant squawking. You tune into the bird and she shows you that her cage used to be in the kitchen and she was much happier there. You tell your friend this, only to find that she recently moved the bird into the living room and that was when the squawking began.

For easy referral I have listed some basic steps that can assist you in telepathic communication.

RESPECT all life.

BELIEVE in your own ability to communicate telepathically with animals.

CENTER or quiet yourself. Take a few deep breaths; practice meditation.

GIVE YOUR ANIMAL FRIEND YOUR FULL ATTENTION. Be mindful in the moment and attentive to the being you are communicating with.

PICTURE YOUR QUESTION or communication in your mind's eye.

SEND THAT PICTURE OR QUESTION mentally to your friend.

RELAX AND ACCEPT whatever communication you receive, whether it is a thought, idea, feeling, or image.

ACKNOWLEDGE that you received the communication. Thank your animal friend.

Animals have so much to share. Open yourself to the possibility. It is time to rejoin our family and our connection with all of life. We are all here on a journey to experience life on our Mother Earth. No "body" is greater than another, simply another way to experience life. They are we and we are they, only in another form. To see God or the Great Spirit in all of life brings us back to completeness. May you walk in balance and harmony, and may you know love.

For information on workshops, lectures,
or other events, please write:

Patty Summers
P.O. Box 275
Evington, VA 24550

or check out her website at

www.heartspace.com/Anicom/index.htm

Hampton Roads Publishing Company

. . .for the evolving human spirit

Hampton Roads Publishing Company
publishes books on a variety of subjects including
metaphysics, health, complementary medicine,
visionary fiction, and other related topics.

For a copy of our latest catalog,
call toll-free, 800-766-8009,
or send your name and address to:

Hampton Roads Publishing Company
134 Burgess Lane
Charlottesville, VA 22902
e-mail: hrpc@hrpub.com
www.hrpub.com